LEADERSHIP STYLES AND
COMPANIES' SUCCESS IN
INNOVATION AND
JOB SATISFACTION

A CORRELATIONAL STUDY

Dr. Israel Agodu

LEADERSHIP STYLES AND COMPANIES' SUCCESS
IN INNOVATION AND JOB SATISFACTION
A CORRELATIONAL STUDY

iUniverse books may be ordered through booksellers or by contacting:

iUniverse
1663 Liberty Drive
Bloomington, IN 47403
www.iuniverse.com
1-800-Authors (1-800-288-4677)

Because of the dynamic nature of the Internet, any web addresses or links contained in this book may have changed since publication and may no longer be valid. The views expressed in this work are solely those of the author and do not necessarily reflect the views of the publisher, and the publisher hereby disclaims any responsibility for them.

Any people depicted in stock imagery provided by Getty Images are models, and such images are being used for illustrative purposes only. Certain stock imagery © Getty Images.

ISBN: 978-1-5320-7751-7 (sc)
ISBN: 978-1-5320-7752-4 (e)

Print information available on the last page.

iUniverse rev. date: 06/20/2019

ABSTRACT

The purpose of this book was to understand the effect of leadership style on employee innovation and job satisfaction as indicators of organizational success in companies that have been in business for more than 10 years. And to ascertain if there is a particular leadership style used by leaders of XYZ retail industry organizations that have been in business for more than 10 years by encouraging and promoting employee innovation and job satisfaction. Investigation hinged primarily on information collected via the Statistics Canada's Survey of Innovation and Business Strategy (SIBS) which measures innovation and the Multifactor Leadership Questionnaires (MLQ) that measures leadership styles and job satisfaction was given to 110 managers and human resource personnel who were chosen at random from the XYZ organization. Mind Garden was used to administer the MLQ 5x-Short survey while Survey Monkey was used to administer innovation assessments. Correlational analysis was employed to assess results from two research questions and four hypotheses. Results provided evidence of significant relationships between transformational leadership style and job satisfaction, $F (3, 71) = 7.627$, $p < .001$, $R^2 = .244$, adj. $R^2 = .212$. The results also demonstrated a significant positive relationship between transformational leadership style and employee innovation in samples of the companies that have been in business for more than 10 years, $f(3, 72) = 77.620$, $p < .001$, $R^2 = 0.764$, adjusted $R^2 = 0.754$. Recommendations are offered to examine these relationships in big organizations to validate the current study using a qualitative or mixed research method.

DEDICATION

I devote this book to the loving memory of my beloved mother, Eulina "Mgbafor" Agodu, who gave me encouragement, commitment, and promise to see me through primary and secondary school after losing her beloved husband early in her married life and the arduous task of raising seven children thereafter. You transitioned into eternal life on August 13, 1998 and did not see the completion of this work. Mother, I celebrate the completion of this journey in honor of you and the excellent gift that you were. Your encouragement and words of wisdom continue to guide and motivate me. Your abiding faith in God has taught me many truths and has produced a source of strength to me, particularly during difficult times. I miss you so much; I know deep in my heart that you are watching over me and cheering me on, just as you promised you would. I love you always. And to my beautiful, supportive, and hard-working wife, Evangelist Angela "Ije'm" Agodu, who supported me emotionally and temporarily suspended her dream of becoming a nurse practitioner to make sure I complete this task. I love you and always will.

ACKNOWLEDGEMENTS

The encouragement and support of many who worked behind the scene have enabled me to actualize this amazing dream. I, first, must thank my daughters (Chidera Sandra Agodu and Chinonso Agodu) and my sons (Chimezie Will Agodu and Odinakachukwu Nathan Agodu) who were with me through this entire journey from start to finish. I love you all for the encouragement, inspiration, support, love, and most importantly, your patience! Second, I wish to appreciate my course mates, Simone Arnold, Cheryl Black, and James Rankin, our collaboration, and encouragements to one another were the motor that brought this task to a successful end.

TABLE OF CONTENTS

LIST OF FIGURES

LIST OF TABLES

CHAPTER 1

INTRODUCTION

Leadership and innovation are essential elements for the development and maintenance of strong and competitive organization (Bowonder, Dambal, Kumar, & Shirodkar, 2010). Leadership is paramount to human existence (Wren, 1995). Leadership is not a fetish, but a practice that is both prehistoric and contemporary (Wren, 1995). Hogan and Kaiser (2005) determined that leadership is significant and crucial for organizational performance. "Leadership is an adaptive tool for individual and group survival; it primarily concerns building and maintaining effective teams: persuading people to give up, for a while, their selfish pursuits and pursue a common goal" (Hogan & Kaiser, 2005, p.170).

Today's business world is intensely competitive; therefore, maintaining a sustainable competitive advantage is crucial to the longevity and success of companies, corporations, and organizations. For this reason, successful business leaders endeavor to epitomize features that create or enhance success and growth. Thus, most business leaders today understand the significance of effective leadership and its influence on productivity and employee loyalty and retention. A strong or weak leader has a tremendous impact on organizational outcomes (Schommer-Aikins & Hutter, 2002).

In this quantitative correlational study, the focal point of the investigation is leadership style, innovation and job satisfaction to ascertain if there is a particular leadership style employed by leaders of XYZ retail industry organizations that have thrived in companies that have been in

1

business for more than 10 years. The aim is to investigate if a correlation exists between leadership style, and innovation and job satisfaction as indicators of success in companies that have been in business for more than 10 years.

One of the enormous challenges confronting CEOs is the ability to bridge the gap between leadership practice and results (Eklund, 2015). Shareholders are less tolerant to failure now than in the past (Eklund, 2015). Between 1997 and 2006, the average term in office for chief executive officers (CEOs) in the United States dropped from ten to eight years; 40% of chief executive officers with the shortest term in office had less than two years in that position due to lack of tolerance for failure (Eklund, 2015).

BACKGROUND

Leadership is one of the major factors that determines the success or failure of any organization (Ojukuku, Odetayo, & Sajuvigbe, 2012). Leadership style drives success, accountability, and organizational performance (Bowonder et al., 2010). Top executives are held responsible for the success or failure of organizations, as well as for designing conditions that guarantee organization's future survival (Ojukuku et al., 2012). Businesses need leaders who understand how to tackle organizational issues and how to work with culturally diverse employees and customers. Strategic decisions often fail due to top executives' mistakes. Top executives fail when: (a) their personal interests interfere with their vision for the organization; (b) they are involved in, or accept, unethical behavior; (c) they have disregard for quality, innovation and productivity, depending too much on intuition to the detriment of logical analysis; or(d) they allocate money and time injudiciously or irresponsibly (Gurdjian, Halbeisen, & Lane, 2014). Gurdjian et al. (2014) forecasted that one-fifth of chief executive officers will resign or be displaced from their position in the next five years. A critical need exists to understand the type of leadership employed by successful chief executive officers and its effect on organizational success. Such knowledge may bring about strong employee benefits such as innovation and job satisfaction, as well as an increase in productivity, growth, expansion, and corporate longevity.

PROBLEM STATEMENT

Presently, limited empirical evidence is available delineating the dominant leadership style used in companies that have been in business for more than 10 years (Schin & Racovita, 2013). Sustained, successful organizations are guided by strong leaders who have the ability to come up with new ideas to keep products, services, and operations fresh (Bowonder et al., 2010). Much study has been carried out globally on the effectiveness of transformational and transactional leadership styles (Schin & Racivita, 2013), but existing studies on leadership have mainly focused on leadership practices and their impact on employee performance, productivity, retention, or commitment. However, little research has been conducted on the effectiveness of dominant styles to influence indicators of organizational success such as employee innovation and job satisfaction (Schin & Racovita, 2013).

General problem. The general problem is retail industry organizations that have not been in business for more than 10 years continues to struggle, despite a plethora of information regarding the importance of leadership styles (transformational, transactional, and laissez-faire), and the effects on innovation and job satisfaction (Ojukuku et al., 2012).

Specific problem. The specific problem is that retail industry organizational leaders do not understand the effect of leadership style on innovation and job satisfaction as indicators of success in companies that have been in business for more than 10 years (Bowonder, Dambal, Kumar, & Shirodkar, 2010). Many studies on different leadership styles have been conducted (Bhatti, Nawab, & Akbar, 2011; Schin, & Racovita, 2013), only a few have been able to demonstrate the effectiveness of leadership practice (transformational, transactional, laissez-faire) and none have been able to pinpoint the dominant style used by leaders to successfully promote and improve employee innovation and job satisfaction within the retail industry (Schin & Racovita, 2013).

Presently, limited empirical evidence is available delineating the dominant leadership style used in companies that have been in business for more than 10 years (Schin, & Racovita, 2013). Organizations have invested money and time in improving the capabilities of leaders. American organizations alone expend nearly $14 billion per annum on leadership initiatives (Gurdjian et al., 2014). Universities and colleges provide dozens of degree programs on leadership, and the price of personalized leadership improvement programs from renowned business schools can surpass $160,000 per student (Gurdjian et al., 2014). In a comparative study carried out in 2014 by Gurdjian et al., 500 chief executive officers (CEOs) were requested to rank their top three human capital priorities. The researchers found that leadership was one of the highest-ranking priorities among CEOs. Sixty-seven percent (2/3) of the executives identified leadership as their biggest concern (Gurdjian et al., 2014). One social and economic consequence of ineffective leadership is workplace conflict between employees and their superiors because it creates disaffection for all parties (Mayhew, 2014). According to Naismith, Sethi, Hoseini, and Tookey (2016), conflict consumes 42% of employee's time and leaders spend 20% of their time in conflict resolution, and over 65% of performance mishaps stem from troubled relationships between employees and leaders. Naismith, Sethi, Hoseini, and Tookey discovered that more than two-thirds of leaders spent over 10% of their time with work-related conflict instead of training employees on innovation that would make their jobs more fulfilling.

PURPOSE STATEMENT

The purpose of this quantitative correlational study was to investigate if a correlation exists between leadership style, innovation and job satisfaction as indicators of organizational success in companies that have been in business for more than 10 years. And to ascertain if there was a dominant leadership style used by leaders of XYZ retail industry organizations that have been in business for more than 10 years. Many studies on different leadership styles have been conducted (Bhatti, Nawab, & Akbar, 2011; Schin, & Racovita, 2013; Ojukuku et al., 2012; Bowonder et al., 2010), only a few have been able to demonstrate the effectiveness of leadership practice (transformational, transactional, laissez-faire, and none have been able to pinpoint the dominant style used by leaders to successfully promote and improve employee innovation and job satisfaction within the retail industry (Schin & Racovita, 2013; Bhatti, Nawab, & Akbar, 2011; Eklund, 2015). Livingston (2003) contributed to the body of knowledge surrounding leadership style and noted the conceptual similarities in transformational and transactional leadership styles, yet correlation between leadership style and organizational success has not yet been conclusively proven.

GENERAL STUDY SIGNIFICANCE

This study was important for several reasons. First, understanding the relationship between leadership style and organizational success using the Multifactor Leadership Questionnaire (MLQ 5x-Short; Avolio & Bass, 2004) and the Statistics Canada's Survey of Innovation and Business Strategy (SIBS) may expound the underlying logic of organizational activities to help organization members evaluate workplace strategies that lead to organizational success. School administrators might use the research findings to design professional development initiatives. Instructors might use the research findings to plan for students with different learning styles. Human resource management can develop retention strategies to keep competent, knowledgeable and experienced employees.

SIGNIFICANCE FOR LEADERSHIP

Leadership usually works with policies and creates rules and regulations. Examining the correlation between the leadership styles, innovation, employee satisfactions and organizational success may suggest the best leadership style that may enhance success in companies that have been in business for more than 10 years. The knowledge may enhance the creation and advancement of innovations that organizations need to maintain and remain competitive. Secondly, understanding the dominant leadership style adopted by some successful leaders in their various organizations could be an invaluable asset to millions of leaders worldwide. The results could help organizational leaders embrace knowledge creation through teamwork, corporate involvement, and information sharing both within and outside the organization as well as guiding organizations in the selection and retention of key personnel. It may bring about the implementation of effective management programs of the selection of leaders who can make use of effective leadership style in the workplace.

NATURE OF THE STUDY

The researcher must decide the type of research design required to answer the problem (Leedy & Ormrod, 2010). A quantitative correlational research method and experimental design were two methods considered appropriate design to achieve the study purpose and address the study problem. However, quantitative correlational research design was the preferred choice for this study because the data consisted of validated numeric measures with no manipulation of variables. When researchers decide that their research problem and questions should be better addressed using quantitative methods, they should choose a design from the four primary approaches suitable for conducting research in the quantitative tradition (O'Dwyer & Bernauer, 2014). Those primary approaches include experimental, non-experimental, correlational, and descriptive designs (O'Dwyer & Bernauer, 2014).

A researcher whose research goal was to examine the effect of treatment or intervention on some phenomenon should consider using an experimental design. Similarly, a researcher who intends to explore naturally occurring phenomena, behaviors, or attributes may consider adopting a non-experimental design, where settings and situations cannot be controlled or manipulated. In an experimental design, researchers can manipulate the setting or situation by creating different conditions for research participants (O'Dwyer & Bernauer, 2014).

The goal of a descriptive design was to describe the variables. In a descriptive study, researchers develop comprehensive records and observe many subjects, but cannot make predictions or determine causality; they simply describe the participants and their behaviors. With descriptive design, researchers look at questions of why and how and do not endeavor to find any causes to answer the research question, but mainly seek for understanding or a detailed description. With this design, the researcher used survey, interviews, case study, or observation as techniques for data collection (Knupfer & McLellan, 2001). However, with a correlational design, the goal was to establish that a relationship exists between two or more variables, while not making a determination if one variable cause another (Knupfer & McLellan, 2001). In a correlational study, researchers cannot manipulate any of the variables or put study participants into the level of one variable based on knowledge of the other variable (Curtis, Comiskey, & Dempsey, 2016). With a correlational design, measurements are scrutinized to pinpoint or determine any groups. Though the correlational study does not determine causality, it is suitable for predicting patterns of correlation that exist between the variables and to measure the strength of the correlation.

A quantitative correlational research design was the preferred choice for this study because the data consisted of validated numeric measures with no manipulation of variables. Because of its inability to examine relationships and to determine the strength of the relationship between variables under investigation, a qualitative and descriptive design, experimental and non-experimental were not appropriate investigatory tools for this study (Leedy & Ormrod, 2013). The quantitative correlational method was also suitable because the variables of interest were measured using questionnaires containing Likert-type scales. Participants responded to the questionnaires by e-mail. When a correlation is established, it can be used to make predictions; that is, when a score on one measure is known, it can be used to make an accurate prediction of another measure that is closely related to it (Srivastava, 2015). This approach helped to ascertain if there exist a correlation between leadership style and organizational success and whether there is a particular leadership style employed by leaders of XYZ organizations that have been in business for more than 10 years.

Population and Sample Size. The proposed population of interest for this study was human resource personnel and managers aged 25-65 years. The population consisted of men and women who have been in their current leadership positions for more than five years. These individuals of interest comprised the target population which set the boundary for the study. From the population of 122 members of two small retail companies, the minimum sample size of 76 individuals was obtained using Soper (2015) Statistics calculators: Version 3.0.

Anticipated effect size (f^2):	0.15
Desired statistical power level:	0.8
Number of predictors:	3
Probability level:	0.05

Minimum required sample size: 76

Data Collection Instruments. The instruments used for this correlational study were the Multifactor Leadership Questionnaire (MLQ-5x) (Avolio & Bass, 2004), and the Statistics Canada's Survey of Innovation and Business Strategy (SIBS). The SIBS was used to provide data on innovation. The survey was comprehensive and required employees (participants) to furnish information on the number of new or improved products, marketing innovation, and the percentage of expenses allocated toward innovation (Statistic Canada's Survey of Innovation, 2012).

Numerous researchers have attested the effectiveness of the MLQ (Gillespie & Mann, 2004). The MLQ model has undergone a series of upgrades, to mitigate imperfections (Avolio & Bass, 2004). Schin and Racivita (2013), and Ojukuku (2012) research also confirm Avolio and Bass's version of the MLQ model as a multicultural tool for acquiring a wide range of leadership conducts, and at the same token isolating or separating effective from ineffective leaders. The investigation relied on information collected via the SIBS and MLQ 5x-short survey given to 110 human resource personnel and managers who were chosen at random (the sample size was validated with a power analysis conducted in G*Power). The MLQ is one of the most commonly used tools for assessing leadership styles and effects. The study was scheduled for a duration period of three to five months.

Data Analysis Approach. The data analysis approach was IBM® SPSS® Statistical Analysis Program Version 24 (IBM, 2016) which would reveal the kind of relationships that exist among variables, disclosing patterns and trends, and allowing researchers to compare the average between the groups in a study to determine whether the means are statistically significantly incompatible to each other (Greenland, Senn, Rothman, Carlin, Poole, Goodman & Altman, 2016).

RESEARCH QUESTIONS AND HYPOTHESES

The research questions narrow the purpose statement down to a question or questions to be answered in the study, thereby enabling researchers to tackle the subject under investigation effectively (Curtis, Comiskey, & Dempsey, 2016). The development of a research question and a supportive hypothesis is an essential step, and a precise research question drives the investigation and the implementation of the study (Farrugia, Petrisor, Farrokhyar, & Bhandari et al., 2010).

RQ1. What is the relationship between leadership style and job satisfaction in companies that have been in business for more than 10 years?

$H1_a$: Leadership style will be positively associated with job satisfaction in companies that have been in business for more than 10 years?

$H1_0$: Leadership style will not be positively associated with job satisfaction in companies that have been in business for more than 10 years?

RQ2. What is the relationship between leadership style and innovation in companies that have been in business for more than 10 years?

$H2_a$: Leadership style will be positively associated with innovation in companies that have been in business for more than 10 years.

$H2_0$ Leadership style will not be positively associated with innovation in companies that have been in business for more than 10 years.

THEORETICAL FRAMEWORK

Leadership literature abounds; leadership and organizational performance, and leadership effectiveness have been examined (Bhatti, Nawab, & Akbar, 2011; Collins, Gibson, Quigley, & Parter, 2016; Schin & Racovita, 2013). Transformational and transactional leadership effectiveness has been studied in the United States and around the world; however, little empirical evidence is available that delineates the dominant style for organizational success (Schin & Racovita, 2013). Livingston (2003) noted the conceptual similarities in transformational and transactional leadership styles, and underscored the gaps existent between transformational, transactional, and laissez-faire styles, but did not draw conclusions about one dominant style associated with organizational success. Therefore, the dearth of information related to leadership style and organizational success constitutes a gap in understanding about how leadership style influences factors such as innovation and employee job satisfaction that indicate organizational success.

This study was an exploration of the correlation between leadership styles and organizational success that is measured by innovation and employee job satisfaction to ascertain whether there is a particular leadership style employed by leaders of XYZ organization who have been in business for more than 10 years, and thus, would add to the body of knowledge on leadership practices (figure 1). This quantitative correlational

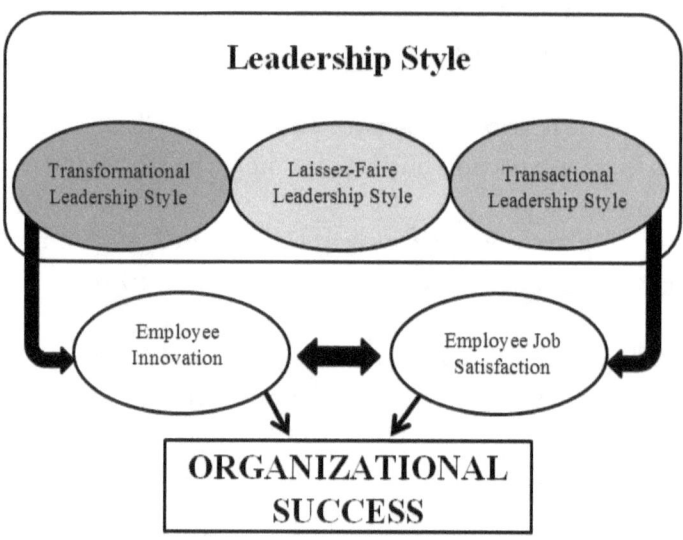

Figure 1: Theoretical framework

study relied on the extensive literature on leadership practices and theories of leadership to test the proposed hypotheses (Curtis, Comiskey, & Dempsey, 2016). The following theories and models should inform the study: transformational leadership theory (Bass & Avolio, 1995); transactional leadership theory (House, Wright, & Adity, 1997); contingency theory (Fielder & Garcia, 1987); laissez-faire leadership (Avolio & Bass, 2004); and situational leadership model (Blanchard, Hersey, & Johnson, 2008); McGregor's (1960) X-Y theory, path-goal theory (Wren, 1995), and behavioral approach (Denison, Hoijberg, & Quinn, 1995) served as an additional guiding framework., McGregor's Theory X (autocratic) leaders embrace the use of force to motivate employees to produce at a higher level while Theory-Y (leaders) encourage, empower, are friendly, imaginative, and creativity driven, Theory-Y leaders believe subordinates need little or no direction, are reliable, hardworking, and know what to do (McGregor, 1960). Path-goal theory of leadership broadly infers leader-structuring behavior will have the most positive impacts on followers' mental states when the followers' duties are ambiguous and strenuous - that is, unstructured (Wren, 1995). The clarity furnished by the leader assists in defining the path to the goal for subordinates. Path-goal theory suggests that only the followers' attributes, and the quality of factors of the work situation, determine which leadership practice will be more effective. Additionally, behavioral theory maintains that a leader's rate of success depends largely on the leader's behavior (Denison et al., 1995).

DEFINITIONS OF TERMINOLOGY

The following key terms used throughout this study are provided. The functional definitions are in line with the focus of the study and the theoretical framework.

Active participation by exception. Active participation by exception is the kind of participation where leaders pay close attention to the needs of others; manage employee performance, and respond to impending problems (Johnson, 2017).

Autocratic leadership. Autocratic leadership is a form of leadership style where leaders possess complete authority and make decisions alone without consulting or seeking others' input (Johnson, 2017).

Charismatic leader. A charismatic leader is a leader who exhibits behaviors or actions that bring about trust and respect, shows concern in the welfare of others, remains composed in disastrous situations, devises strategy that is beneficial to the entire group, shows competence, and gains subordinates' respect (Bass & Avolio, 1994).

Chief Executive Officer (CEO). The chief executive officer is the highest- ranking corporate position; CEOs are responsible for the day-to-day operational activities of an organization and set the tone and direction for an organization to follow (Parand, Dopson, & Vincent, 2013).

Constructive motivation. Constructive motivation is the ability of the leader to arouse and captivate followers by providing challenging and meaningful tasks, urging followers to do more for the good of everyone in the organization (Bass, 1985).

Contingent reward. Contingent reward is a technique used by leaders to reward employees for attaining or not attaining work objectives (Bass, 1985).

Dominant leadership style. A dominant leadership style is the style considered by the leader to be the best approach for motivating employees and increasing productivity.

Hands-off approach. Hands-off approach is an approach where leaders do not manage employee performance and do not respond to problems (Bass, 1985).

Innovation. Innovation is an improvement in the organization or processes within the organization; the transformation of a new idea into a new product or service (Heye, 2006).

Intellectual stimulation. Intellectual stimulation is when leaders encourage individual problem-solving and decision making and promote risk taking by letting subordinates develop multiple ways to approach existing organizational problems or issues (Kirkbride, 2006).

Laissez-faire leadership. Laissez-faire leadership is the kind of leadership where leaders employ a hands-off approach and allow workers to make decisions concerning their work (Avolio & Bass, 2004).

Leadership. Leadership is a process of transforming followers by creating visions, goals, and the path for followers to accomplishing the goals (Bass, 1985).

Participative leadership. Participative leadership is a leadership style where leaders value teamwork and followers' involvement in the decision making. Participative leaders stimulate and enhance employees' morale, making employees feel valued and relevant (Johnson, 2017).

Passive participation by exception. Passive participation by exception happens when a leader becomes involved in the affairs of the organization only when error is perceived or detected (Bass, 1985).

Personalized reflection. Personalized reflection is a leader's self-discovery in which the leader recognizes personal flaws as well as strengths. This type of reflection is a key to understanding others (House, Wright, & Aditya, 1997).

Transformational leadership style. A transformational leadership style is where a leader works with his or her team members to create common goals that are informed by the shared collection of ideas (Bass, 1990).

Transactional leadership. Transactional leadership style is a kind of leadership style where leaders make certain that the route to task accomplishments is intelligibly followed by followers, to eliminate impending hindrance and inspire followers to fulfill the prearranged goals (House, Wright, & Aditya, 1997).

Table 1
Operational Variables

Construct	Variables	Cause/Predictor (Effect/Criterion)
Transformational leadership	Transformational leadership	Cause/Predictor (independent)
Transactional leadership	Transactional leadership	Cause/Predictor (Independent)
Laissez-faire Leadership	Laissez-faire leadership	Cause/Predictor (Independent)
Organizational success	Innovation	Effect/Criterion(dependent)
Organizational success	Job satisfaction	Effect/Criterion(dependent)

CONTRIBUTIONS TO KNOWLEDGE

This study was motivated by a need to understand which leadership style is most effective for organizational success. Thus, understanding the relationship between organizational success and leadership style using the MLQ-5x and SIBS may help leaders and organizations explore the underlying logic of organizational activities and help organization members evaluate performance. This understanding may enhance the creation and advancement of innovations that organizations need to maintain and remain competitive. Second, understanding the dominant leadership style adopted by some successful leaders in their various organizations could be an invaluable asset to millions of leaders worldwide. The results could help companies embrace knowledge creation through teamwork, corporate involvement, and information sharing both within and outside the organization.

EXTENSION OF THEORY AND PRACTICE

The more human beings understand about themselves, the more control they have over their own destiny (Tsoukas, 2005). Many leaders and organizations have realized that to function effectively today; they must become knowledge-based. Knowledge is a source of a sustainable superior business position that allows for the creation of values for the next generation of successful individuals, groups, and organizations (Nonaka & Nishiguchi, 2001). The outcome of this study may provide reliable and useful information for leaders. The results may strengthen the breadth of leadership as a branch of knowledge and produce positive scholarly insight into effective leadership methods. The results may also provide suggestions for avenues by which organizations can receive more from their leadership initiative efforts. Such insight would positively influence how organizations and their leaders address pressures stemming from the need to globalize, ever-evolving technological developments, and continued macroeconomic unpredictability (Gurdjian et al., 2014).

ASSUMPTIONS

The primary assumption surrounding this study was that employee innovation would be high in companies that thrive, indicating organizational success. Employee job satisfaction would be high in companies that thrive, indicating organizational success. Employee innovation would be low in companies that fail, indicating a lack of organizational success. Employee job satisfaction would be low in companies that fail, indicating a lack of organizational success. Additionally, the managers and human resource personnel of the XYZ organization would voluntarily participate in the study and honestly and professionally give their best responses to the questionnaire. It was also assumed that these individuals would be anxious and eager to participate due to the study's impending significance to leadership and knowledge advancement. Using research to establish the relationship between leadership style and organizational success may boost CEO performance as well as employer and employees' satisfaction.

Similarly, it was assumed that the participants would map out enough time to enable the completion of the survey in one setting with limited disruptions and would allow the researcher to solely control the generalizability of the study. It was also assumed that participants would participate voluntarily and freely without an expectation for remuneration or incentives. The problem and purpose statement of the study would serve as encouragement and motivational tools that may convince them to participate.

SCOPE

The scope of the study was an assessment of the correlation between leadership styles of top executives of the XYZ organization that have been in business for more than 10 years, and to ascertain if they use a specific leadership style to make their organizations successful. Managers and human resource personnel are in a position that helps determine the vision, mission, and best leadership practices of the organization that maximize market share and get the best effort from the employees (Bass, 1985). The study investigated the leadership styles of CEOs of the XYZ organization through the questionnaires that was given to their various managers and human resource personnel.

LIMITATIONS

A potential limitation of this study was the loss of participants. This loss could occur when managers or human resource personnel who established sound rapport with the researcher, and willingly volunteered to participate, exited the position by resignation or retirement, and were replaced by new and incoming managers or human resource personnel at the time the survey started. The study would be affected if those new and incoming managers and human resource personnel were asked to participate but declined due to a lack of an established rapport with the researcher.

Another limitation could be that managers or human resource personnel, who originally agreed to participate before the surveys were emailed, chose not to participate before the start of the survey. The study might be affected because it might reduce the sample size of the study. There was also the likelihood that some managers and human resource personnel might not be reached due to their busy work schedules. Also, managers for whom English is a second language may not interpret the questions like those for whom English is a primary language. This could affect the generalizability of the results. Other limitations that may threaten the internal and external validity of the survey could be participants' mood on the day of the survey, if the participant was disgruntled about something or someone, he or she may interpret the questions through that emotional lens.

DELIMITATIONS

Delimitations are used to reduce the scope of the study or to itemize what is not covered or deliberated in the study (Leedy & Ormrod, 2013). The first delimitation was that the study only included managers and human resource personnel of the XYZ organization. The second delimitation was that it only involved the leadership styles of top executives that may affect organizational success. The third delimitation relates to the variables under investigation and their various characteristics. These include transformational leadership style, transactional leadership style, and laissez-faire leadership style. Other variables such as corruption, acquisition/merger, and cyber-security that affect organizational success were identified but not measured.

Summary

Chapter 1 supplied a detailed background analysis considered relevant to the study's problem, purpose statement, and general significance, as well as significance for leadership. The chapter also deliberated on the nature of the problem, research questions, hypotheses, and the conceptual framework. The chapter concluded with the definition of terms, followed by a short discussion on the scope, delimitations, and limitations of the study. The outcome of any organization depends largely on the leader's suitability to harness and make the most out of human resources. In this ever-changing environment, top executives worldwide are being challenged to make a viable connection between leadership practice and results, situating, stimulating or energizing, and empowering the organization to follow through on their strategic roadmap. Leadership style can impact organizational success (Bass & Avolio, 1994). Many CEOs who are terminated are not dismissed due to a lack of vision, but rather from failure to engage their own organization in well-defined leadership practices (Ekelund, 2015).

The theoretical framework for this study embraced transformational, transactional, and laissez-faire leadership styles. The purpose of this quantitative correlational research was to examine leadership style and to determine if there exists a particular leadership style employed by leaders of XYZ organization who have been in business for more than 10 years. The investigation hinged primarily on information collected via the SIBS, and MLQ given to 110managers and human resource personnel who were chosen at random based on the number of dependent variables by the researcher. A quantitative method was selected over a qualitative method because of the quantitative method's ability to evaluate the strength of the correlation between variables under investigation (Leedy & Ormrod, 2013).

CHAPTER 2

LITERATURE REVIEW

Chapter 2 begins with a recap of the questions that drove the study followed by the search strategy and literature review process. The chapter ends with a conclusion and summary. This correlational study was conducted to ascertain answers to two questions: First, what is the relationship between leadership style and job satisfaction in companies that have been in business for more than 10 years? Second, what is the relationship between leadership style and innovation in companies that have been in business for more than 10 years? The goal of this quantitative correlational study was to investigate if a correlation exists between leadership style, innovation and job satisfaction as indicators of success in companies that have been in business for more than 10 years. The study also ascertained if there exists a particular leadership style employed by leaders of XYZ retail industry organizations that have been in business for more than 10 years by encouraging and promoting innovation while other companies in the same retail industry have failed.

SEARCH STRATEGY/DOCUMENTATION

The relevant literature was scrutinized from professional peer-reviewed journals and dissertations from the University of Phoenix Library. The audit included Internet searches of websites and databases including EBSCOhost, Info Trac, ProQuest, ProQuest Dissertations and Theses, and Thomas Gale Power Search. Mind Garden Incorporated furnished information on the Multifactor Leadership Questionnaire survey tool, while a Google search elicited information about the Statistics Canada's Survey of Innovation and Business Strategy (SIBS). A total of 85 dissertations and journal articles, 31Internet sites, 30 books, and one encyclopedia provided information on the leadership style, innovation, job satisfaction, survey tools, quantitative research method and design as well as instruments that were relevant to the study (Table 2).

Table 2
Sources Consulted for the Literature Review

Publication Type	Total	Pre 2010	2010 or later
Internet	31	11	20
Dissertation	10	0	10
Books	30	10	20
Journals	75	31	44
Encyclopedia	1	1	0
Total	147	53	94

To address the issue of leadership style, literature search was conducted in the areas of leadership, active participation, emotional intelligence (EI), motivation, organizational performance, innovation, and job satisfaction. The literature search included an exploration of relevant leadership theories, such as transformational leadership theory (Bass & Avolio1994), transactional leadership theory (House & Adity, 1997), contingency theory (Fieldler & Garcia, 1987), Theory of X-Y (McGregor, 1960), behavioral approach (Denison et al., 1995), path goal theory (Wren, 1995), and trait theory (Fleenor, 2011).

HISTORICAL PERSPECTIVE OF LEADERSHIP THEORY

Leadership isparamount to human existence (Wren, 1995). Leadership is not a fetish, but a practice that is both prehistoric and contemporary (Wren, 1995). Hogan and Kaiser (2005) determined that leadership is significant and crucial for organizational performance. "Leadership is an adaptive tool for individual and group survival; it primarily concerns building and maintaining effective teams: persuading people to give up, for a while, their selfish pursuits and pursue a common goal" (Hogan & Kaiser, 2005, p.170).

Theories are developed in association with time and space as factors. Therefore, it is apparent that this may be a gray area involving both new theory construction and derivation techniques from existing theories. Through re-traceability over the last four decades, it is apparent that theory development is ongoing as knowledge is expanded. Thus, transformational leadership (Figure 2) and transactional leadership (Figure 3) were the main theories guiding the study; other theories (Figure 4) were considered in order to inform the author's comprehension of leadership.

Transformational theory of leadership. Transformational leadership is associated with innovation in organizations (Bowonder et al., 2010). Transformational leadership allows followers to ascend to the highest extent of fulfillment than believed practicable. Transformational leadership behaviors elevate followers' dedication toward supporting the leader's dream, assuming more responsibility, creating innovative techniques, and performing more efficiently (Bowonder et al., 2010). Leaders who employ a transformational approach do not dwell on an individual, but on the alliance that exists among individuals. Transformational leaders encourage and energize followers to attain excellent outcomes and in so doing, expand leader's leadership capability (Hickman, 2016). Transformational leaders assist followers to develop and sprout into leaders by paying attention to their needs, empowering, and aligning the goals and objectives of each person, the group, the leader, and the larger organization (Hickman, 2016, p. 76). Transformational leadership's focal point is to transform human circumstance that can spring forth from any source. It permits individuals from every department in an organization to assume leadership roles.

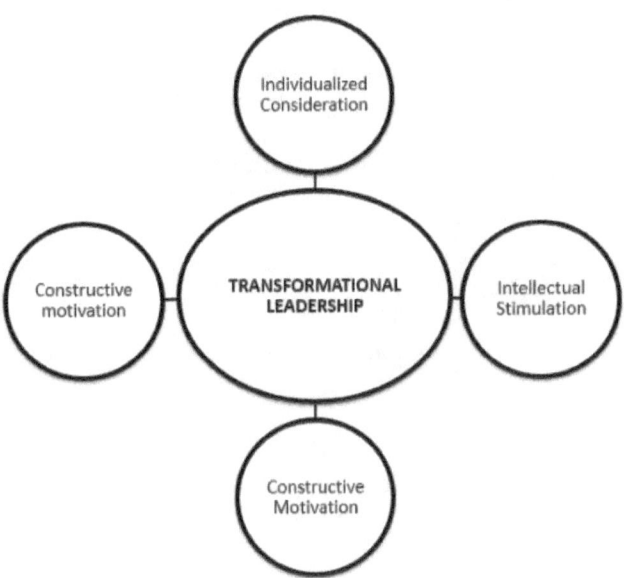

Figure 2. Characteristics of Transformational Leadership

Hickman (2016) submitted that transformational leaders encourage, motivate, and empower followers by aligning the goals and objectives of individual followers, the group, the leader, and the entire organization. Transformational leaders exhibit particular behaviors and attributes such as charisma, intellectual stimulation, constructive motivation, and personalized reflection (Figure 2).

Charisma. Attributed charisma happens anytime leaders exhibit actions or behaviors that bring about trust and respect. Leaders who exhibit charisma show concern for the welfare of others, remain composed in disastrous situations, and devise a strategy that will be beneficial to the entire group (Bass & Avolio, 1994). They also show competence and gain followers' respect as they discharge their duties (Bass & Avolio, 1994).

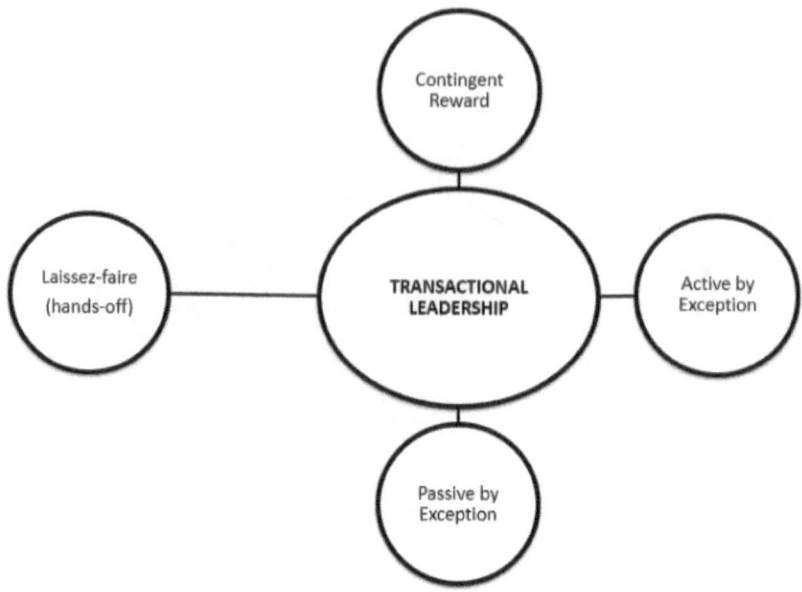

Figure 3. Characteristics of Transactional Leadership

Constructive motivation. Leaders who use constructive motivation arouse and captivate followers by providing challenging and meaningful tasks (Hickman, 2015). Motivational leaders are good at convincing followers through actions and deeds that their leadership style is what the organization, as well as everyone working for the organization, needs (Kirkbride, 2006). They can relate to others in a respectful, non-degrading, and non-threatening fashion, as well as give work order directions that are approved by everyone in the organization. Constructive motivation leaders urge followers to do more for the betterment of everyone in the organization. Therefore, followers are ever ready to go above and beyond the call of duty to achieve more for themselves, the group, and the organization, simply because of the leader's action and behavior toward them.

Intellectual stimulation. Transformational leaders encourage intellectual stimulation. Intellectual stimulation includes creativity, a redefinition of problems, risk taking, questioning assumptions, and exploration of multiple approaches to existing problems and methods. Intellectual stimulation is a major attribute of transformational leadership, where the leader encourages individual problem-solving and decision-making (Kirkbride, 2006). The leader promotes risk taking by allowing followers to develop multiple ways of approaching existing organizational problems or issues. The leader might offer some assistance, but employees are left in charge of deciding what and which resources and techniques should be used for the task. A leader who is endowed with intellectual stimulation qualities stimulates the minds and visions of subordinates to formulate new or different ways of getting work accomplished in an effective and efficient fashion. Followers who are under this facet of transformational leadership embrace teamwork and are eager to ask questions and share information to foster innovation in the organization (Kirkbride, 2006).

Individualized consideration. Leaders who employ individual thought form personalized relationships with followers to support and empower them. Transformational leadership behaviors elevate followers' dedication toward supporting the leader's dream, assuming more responsibility, creating innovative techniques, and performing more efficiently (Bass, 1990). A personalized relationship is an essential quality of a leader; the leader shows interest in the personal and professional desires and advancement of followers. The leader makes time to listen to followers, and ensures job allocations are within the range-, ability, and knowledge of the followers. Individualized consideration, also known as personalized relationship/reflection, is an essential characteristic of transformational leadership, where leaders create time to learn and understand followers. Leaders map out time from their busy schedule for information sharing with followers, showing them how much the organization values the followers' input.

Transformational leaders motivate employees and teams to surpass expectations by embracing a vision and aiming to achieve that vision (Bass, 1990). Cognizance of transformational leadership contentions/assumptions by itself is enough for being a successful leader. Sergiovanni (1990) identified 10 transformational leadership behaviors any leader can establish with subordinates: (a) greet - to show employees that their presence at work is valued and appreciated. Leaders should greet employees every day, encourage other employees to do likewise, encourage employees to set goals and objectives; doing so demonstrates to employees that their opinions matter. (b) Show a desire and willingness to listen and incorporate followers' input. (c) Advise employees to search for new and alternative solutions by welcoming and encouraging different viewpoints. (d) Do not encourage "status-quo thinking." (e) Dare employees to expand their innate intellectual and creative abilities and avoid infringing on personal points of view. (f) Use a participatory leadership technique. (g) Clarify and summarize main points during meetings. (h) Assign tasks and involve employees in administrative activities by initiating the teams and demonstrating how power should be distributed. (i) Openly appreciate followers and teams who have added to the organization's objectives in various departments and capacities; and finally. (j) Encourage employees to attempt different ideas and support risk taking.

Transactional theory of leadership. Transactional leadership requires an interchange procedure that brings about follower adherence to leader desire, but is unlikely to produce commitment and enthusiasm to the mission objective (Hickman, 2016). The leader's attention is concentrated on making sure followers discharge duties necessary to accomplish the organization's set goals. The purpose of a transactional leadership is to make certain that the routes to task accomplishment are intelligibly followed by followers, to eliminate impending hindrances, and to inspire subordinates to fulfill the prearranged goals (House et al., 1997). Leaders who practice transactional leadership style provide jobs to perform and incentives for completion, or issue penalties to team members for performance outcomes (Hickman, 2016). Leaders, together with members of the team, set prearranged goals, and followers agree to follow the directives and leadership of the manager to get the job done. The leader has the power to examine outcomes, train, and correct employees whenever team members fail to achieve organization's goals. Subordinates get incentives such as bonuses when they meet identified goals. In contrast to transformational leaders, transactional leaders endeavor to search for followers' self-interests by initiating a conversation link. Hickman (2016) suggested four transactional leadership practices: contingent reward, passive leadership by exception, active leadership by exception, and laissez-faire (Figure 3).

Contingent reward. When employing the contingent reward feature of transactional leadership, the leader establishes a clear expectation and utilizes a "perks" technique to reward followers for attaining work objectives. The leader vigorously observes performance, looking to reward employees who positively provide higher levels of effort and performance. A contingent reward is perceived as a positive and active relationship that exists between leaders and followers where followers are compensated for achieving desired objectives (Howell & Avolio, 1993).

Passive/active leadership by exception. Passive leadership by exception occurs when the leader incorporates negative reinforcement or punishment to counteract mediocrity and unsatisfactory performance (Bass, 1985). The leader gets involved in the affairs of the organization only when an error is perceived or detected. However, in an *active* leadership by exception, leaders pay close attention to the needs of others, manage employee performance, and respond to problems.

Laissez-faire **Leadership.** Laissez-faire leadership style is characterized by the assumption of a hands-off approach. The leader pays no attention to the needs of others, does not manage employee performance, and does not respond to problems (Bass, 1985; Yukl, 2013). Laissez-faire leadership affects others through exchanging work for wages but does not support worker creativity nor does it boost work morale. Yukl (2013) submitted that laissez-faire does not represent leadership because of leaders' avoidance of involvement in conflict resolution, interaction with subordinates, and lack of interest at events around them. Laissez-faire leaders are unapproachable and believe that employees are capable of solving problems on their own (Hickman, 2016). Laissez-faire leadership is the perfect opposite of autocratic leadership where a leader makes every decision for a company, team, or group. Laissez-faire leaders make little or no decisions; instead they allow employees to decide on appropriate workplace solutions (Yukl, 2013). Yukl (2013) reasoned that effective leaders encourage group interactions and affect employees' behaviors to achieve organizational goals, but laissez-faire leaders do not offer any assistance to employees; rather, they employ people with experience, good education, and strong skills who are ambitious and driven to succeed, have a track record of achievement on specific projects, and who are comfortable performing tasks with little or no guidance (Gill, 2016).

Contingency approach to leadership. The contingency leadership approach proposes that work group or organizational factors determine the level to which leader

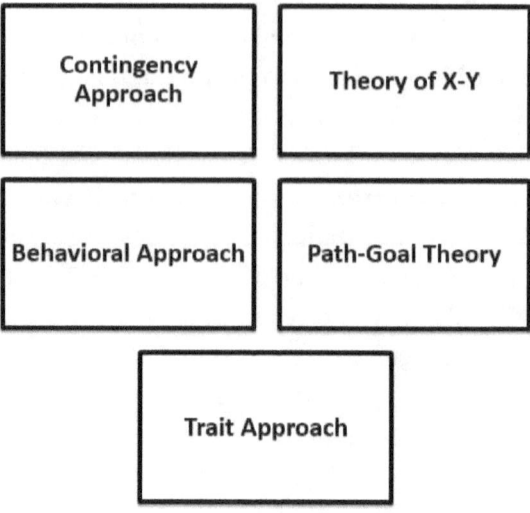

Figure 4. Contributing theories

characteristics and behaviors will be successful (Fiedler& Garcia, 1987). In other words, organizational situation determines the best suitable leadership technique. Contingency theories uphold an if-then relationship between leader and follower; that is, if this is the situation or circumstance, then this is the appropriate leadership practice to be used (Fiedler & Garcia, 1987). Therefore, leaders should be capable of modifying any given phenomenon by incorporating different leadership techniques. The contingency approach is usually arduous to execute in practice, simply because leaders often have one leadership technique that is hard to amend (Fiedler & Garcia, 1987). The most commonly practiced contingency approach is the "situational leadership model." The theory maintains that a leader's style should be modified to align with the follower's ability or competency (Hickman, 2016). For instance, a leader supervising a new employee could apply a directive technique and meticulously monitor the employee. A leader in charge of a knowledgeable and dedicated follower might apply a more emissary style, permitting the employee to make more decisions (Hickman, 2016).

A leader who gives an unfavorable rating to a follower is the kind of person who derives joy from success and pays more attention to success. Such a leader might be labeled, task motivated (YukI, 2013). Any leader who gives a least-preferred follower a passably positive rating would appear to be more worried about the interpersonal aspects of the situation, rather than the task aspects; this type of leader would be deemed, relationship motivated. The task-motivated leader pays more attention to task-related aspects of the leadership situation, is more focused on task success, and under every circumstance, more likely to act in a structuring, directive, and somewhat autocratic way (Hickman, 2016). The "relationship-motivated leader," on the other hand, pays better attention to interpersonal matters, is more focused on evading conflict and preserving high morale, and is more inclined to act with a considerate and participative leadership style (Hickman, 2016). Nevertheless, contingency model studies on the impacts of leadership training have indicated that training has its most powerful impact on a leader's situational control (Hickman, 2016). Training affords leaders the knowledge, procedures, and techniques that ultimately increase a sense of control over the group's activities (Hickman, 2016).

Theory of X-Y. The theory of X-Y (McGregor, 1960) is the basic foundation used to develop and differentiate between management/ leadership techniques. In 1960, McGregor grouped leaders into two unique leadership styles and called them, Theory-X and Theory-Y. Theory-X, an autocratic leadership style, maintains that leaders should apply force to get subordinates to perform at the highest levels, thus prompting theory-X leaders to intently monitor and supervise followers (McGregor, 1960). This leadership practice involves a "my-way-or-the-highway" approach to managing people. Theory-X leaders are result and deadline driven, short tempered, loud, and very demanding, un-sportsman–like, usually do not permit employees to participate in decision-making, or call for their opinion on matters of concern. Theory-X leaders strive for absolute control and have zero concern about subordinates' welfare or morale. They believe employees are unmotivated, do not like working, need direction, need to be controlled and forced, and avoid responsibilities. Theory-Y leaders, also known as democratic or participative leaders, maintain that given the right conditions, people will allocate more time to work just as they would allocate more time to personal activities and leisure (McGregor, 1960). Theory-Y leaders encourage, empower, and are friendly, imaginative, and creativity driven. They believe subordinates need little or no direction, are reliable, hardworking, and know what to do. Theory-Y leaders allow followers or workers to take part in decision-making and seek for their opinions on organizational matters (McGregor, 1960). The theory of X-Y has not only impacted workplace leaders to re-examine the way they conducted organizational affairs previously, but has continued to allow them to analyze and refine their modus operandi to work towards a more Y-based environment.

The behavioral approach. The behavioral approach brings into focus noticeable and perceptible behavior that defines successful leadership (Denison et al., 1995). Fleishman (1953) chronicled the renowned Ohio State University and University of Michigan leadership research of the 1940s and 1950s. In those studies, researchers distributed questionnaires asking participants to rate their superiors on many behavioral issues. Two key behaviors surfaced from this study: task-oriented and people-oriented behaviors (Fleishman, 1953). Task-oriented behaviors entail constructing work tasks and roles, defining work procedures and processes, and making sure that employees adhere to organizational policy, while people-oriented behaviors entail formulating a close and harmonious relationship with employees, showing common respect, involving employees in decision making, and showing concern for employees' welfare (Denison et al., 1995). People-oriented leaders pay more attention to interpersonal relationships. Task-oriented leaders are more concerned with getting the job done. They structure, plan, organize, and strictly supervise workers (Vecchio & Fernandez, 2002). Initially, researchers who carried out these studies concluded that people-oriented and task-oriented styles were incompatible, that a task-oriented leader is autocratic and shows no concern for followers' well-being, while a people-oriented leader concentrates solely on interpersonal relationships. The researchers later deduced that these techniques were not connected to each other; a leader might exhibit high or low aptness in both techniques (Vecchio & Fernandez, 2002).

Path-goal theory. Path-goal theory deals primarily with the significance of leadership conduct and action on subordinate stimulation and contentment instead of the more general issues of performance and decision making. The theory infers "leader-structuring behavior will have the most positive impacts on follower mental states when the follower's duties are ambiguous and strenuous, that is, unstructured" (Wren, 1995, p. 90). The clarity furnished by the leader assists in defining the path to the goal for subordinates (Wren, 1995). Path-goal theory suggests that only the followers' attributes and the qualities or factors of the work situation determine which leadership practice will be more efficient. The theory includes four leadership behaviors: participative leadership, achievement-oriented leadership, supportive, and directive leadership (Yukl, 2013). This theory is not about inclusion in decision making, and might more appropriately be considered a theory of supervision where the leaders have high clarity, and followers support their decisions. A most interesting finding by Hernandez, Eberly, Avolio, and Johnson (2011) indicated that in addition to job features, the followers' needs, attitudes, and expectations have a substantial impact on the followers' reaction to leader behavior. Hernandez et al. (2011) found that leaders who scored high on a measure of desire for personal development preferred not to receive structuring supervision, even under conditions of ambiguity. These subordinates would rather not have higher level oversight of their work.

The trait approach. The trait approach to leadership, deals mainly with the personal attitudes (traits) of leaders such as physical, temperament, worth, and aptitude. It sees leadership purely from an individual's perspective. Pertinent in this approach is the assumption that traits create patterns of conduct that are undeviating in all conditions (Wren, 1995). Leadership quality is regarded to be a lasting characteristic that humans are born with, and that remains somewhat steady for a long time (Fleenor, 2011). Many early researchers considered leadership as a one-dimensional personality trait that could be measured (Fleenor, 2011). They attempted to ascertain the features that separate leaders from followers. In spite of meticulous effort, it was difficult and impracticable to discern traits that usually distinguished a follower from a leader. Leadership characteristics that could make leaders effective included the willingness to lead, perseverance, integrity, self-assurance, intellectual capacity, and experience (Kirkpatrick & Locke, 1991). The trait approach assumes all leaders are created equal; therefore, leaders are endowed with the same personal traits, and a leadership approach that worked in one situation can work in all other situations. The notion that one leadership approach fits every situation is no doubt a false presumption (Yukl, 2013). An assessment of leadership literature revealed references to a variety of traits affiliated with leadership behavior. No individual feature or sets of leadership features have been authenticated as most efficient (Hickman, 2016).

Though, the literature review has revealed that it is difficult and perhaps impracticable to discern traits that distinguish a follower from a leader. And the notion that no one leadership approach fit every situation (Yukl, 2013) makes the study even more significant. It has provided a foundation for the research questions and support for the selected hypotheses, quantitative methodology, multiple regression analysis, and correlational research design. The application of statistical procedures to data analysis will provide an objective method of testing the research hypotheses and a relationship between theory and research (Frankfort-Nachmias & Leon-Guerrero, 2006).

GERMINAL AND CURRENT LITERATURE

Many studies have been carried out globally on the effectiveness of transformational and transactional leadership styles (Schin & Racivita, 2013; Bass, 1999; Bono & Judge, 2004). A wealth of literature that evaluated the relationships between transformational and transactional leadership style and organizational success exists (Bass, 1999). Many also addressed the factors of transactional and transformational leadership styles and their correlations with job satisfaction, retention, empowerment, and job performance in diverse organizational settings (Bono & Judge, 2004; Walumbwa, Orwa, Wang, & Lawler, 2005; Frooman, Mendelson, & Murphy, 2012). Research findings corroborated theoretical assertions that the relationship between transformational and transactional leadership style and results varies in different organizational settings (Howell & Avolio, 1993; Bass, 1990; Judge & Piccolo, 2004; Shamir & Howell, 1999).

Leadership literature embraces empirical studies employing predominantly a quantitative methodology to assess relationships between transactional and transformational leadership style and organizational success. In the present correlational study, transactional, transformational and laissez-faire leadership styles of managers and human resource personnel were the three predictor variables and employee innovation and job satisfaction were the criterion variables. The pertinent sources of the literature comprised studies that dealt with the major variables of the study, transactional, transformational, laissez-faire as well as innovation and job satisfaction.

In a mixed method study, Eisenbeiss, van Knippenberg and Boerner (2008) conducted research to evaluate the relationship between transformational leadership style and team innovation, incorporating team climate principle, the study results furnished evidence of the positive correlation between transformational leadership and team innovation. The qualitative results of the study added to a cavernous comprehension of the correlations between team innovation and transformational leadership (Eisenbeiss et al., 2008). The major demerit of mixed method studies is that they expand the scope of research through utilization of varied methods of inquiry where researchers must report the findings of both quantitative and qualitative research (Curtis, Comiskey, & Dempsey, 2016).

Other pertinent studies employed a quantitative research methodology, which has been predominantly used in the area of industrial and organizational psychology (Rogelberg, 2004). Some of the selected articles were quantitative studies that employed either an experiential design, such as field experiment (Barling, Weber, & Kelloway, 1996), or nonexperimental designs, such as a cross-sectional survey (Leach, 2005), a correlational design (Emery & Barker, 2007), or longitudinal research design (Payne & Huffman, 2005). The experimental research uses random allotment of participants to control groups and manipulate predictor variables to assess their effect on criterion variables, which permits the establishment of cause and effect relationships between variables (Curtis, Comiskey, & Dempsey, 2016).

EFFECTS OF LEADERSHIP STYLE

Leadership paradigms. An organization's success depends largely on the leader's suitability to harness and make the most out of human resources (Ojokuku et al., 2012). Theories of leadership were first developed in the early 1920s, and have evolved at a steady pace over time. Organizations are adjusting to keep up with the evolution of leadership best practices. Some of the ways organizations are evolving into the postmodern world include supporting teamwork, stimulating employees, and welcoming diversity (White & Bruton, 2011). However, many leaders are following old paradigms of leadership (Hickman, 2015). The major distinction between the new and old patterns of leadership centers on involvement, dominance, and stability (Vecchio, 1998). Old-pattern leaders strive for domination and influence. New-pattern leaders strive for involvement, stimulation, and emancipation (Vecchio, 1998).

Practitioners, researchers, and philosophers have addressed the concepts of leadership, comparing and contrasting the differences between modernism and post-modernism approaches (Wren, 1995). These experts believe that effective leadership is fundamental to the survival of organizations but disagree on how that effectiveness should be achieved. Philosophers and researchers like Hogan and Kaiser (2005) argued that leadership is essential for organizational effectiveness. It resolves the problem of how to organize the communal effort. With sound leadership, organizations including hospitals, corporations, governments, armies, and universities flourish and prosper. In essence, good leadership is crucial for obtaining successful work accomplishment and can transform possibilities into actualities (Collins, 2001).

Leader characteristics. Advocates of positivism assert that leaders should think outside the box because there is no one best way of managing people (Collins, 2001; Johns & Duberley, 2001). Positivist epistemology maintains that leaders should intelligibly employ scientifically proven leadership techniques, and that these techniques work in almost every situation (Delanty & Strydom, 2003; Kuhn, 2012). Similarly, Schommer-Aikins and Hunter (2002) maintained that taking alternative approaches or viewpoints, recognizing the difficulty of matters, employing flexible thinking, recognizing that knowledge is always evolving, being inquisitive, and organizing thoughts by planning and thinking ahead are keys to organizational success (Schommer-Aikins & Hunter, 2002, p.3).

Leaders make decisions and influence support and input from others (Greenwald, 2008). To assist with this, leaders may deploy imperative force, reward mechanisms, and impart a culture of shared or common cause with members. Through this three-pronged approach, two distinct forces are noticeable: (a) leaders bring the right people on board, and (b) leaders select actions to achieve goals (Wren, 1995). The following leader attributes are part of the leadership suite of characteristics and behaviors:

- Leaders take and demonstrate initiative.
- Leaders lead by example, exercise oversight, create solutions, identify paths to solutions.
- Leaders connect with stakeholders and strive to maintain relationships inside and outside of the firm.
- Leaders facilitate task and information flow.
- Leaders support and serve as advocates for members' values.
- Leaders add the human element to abstract rules, regulations, and vision.
- Leaders can exercise brute force, tyrannical behaviors, which may disengage followers. Effective leaders collaborate and integrate members.
- Leadership "requires partnership between leaders and followers in a fashion that meets and advances the objective of both" (Greenwald, 2008, p. 226).

According to Collins (2001), great leaders determine the path to attain greatness. Collins explained that the great leaders are those who "got the right people on the bus, the wrong people off the bus, and the right people in the right seats" (Collins, 2001, p. 15). Collins asserted that the right people, not just "people," are the company's most important asset. Collins also explained that a great leader "focuses on getting and hanging on to the right people in the first place – those who are productively neurotic, who are self-motivated and self-disciplined, who wake up every day, compulsively driven to do the best they can because it is simply part of their DNA" (p. 15).

For companies to be effective, leaders must inject a culture of inclusion into the organization, as inclusion paves the way for innovation and knowledge creation that are essential ingredients in the development and maintenance of a strong and competitive organization. Effective leadership is an indispensable prerequisite for collaborative teamwork, innovation, and improved performance in an organization. In today's competitive business arena, the success of any business or organization depends largely on selecting the right technology and right vision for the future (White & Bruton, 2011). Innovation is the great way to achieve success and maintain a competitive edge. According to White and Bruton (2011), in business, leaders must do things smarter, different, or better that makes a favorable difference in value, productivity or quality by making use of emerging or proven technologies. This idea lends support that leaders must be visionary and innovative to adapt to the ever-changing world. For organizations to remain competitive, a leader must be in place to pilot the affairs of the company through vision and innovation (White & Bruton, 2011). The leader accomplishes this task by clearly defining the company's mission, desired results, and most importantly, assessing actions to determine if the behaviors are beneficial, being willing to make necessary adjustments when the need arises (Manning, 2015). For paradigm shift to occur, leaders must support an environment whereby followers can appreciate the direction of the organization and feel part of the process, which will set the stage for better participation and innovation (Kuhn, 2012).

Another factor influencing leadership success is the leader's ability to follow. A good leader knows how to follow others. Leaders and followers are not opposites, but complement each other (Buckingham, 2005). To achieve the highest organizational performance, leaders must not only be able to direct organizational activity, they must be able to concede leadership when the greater good could be served by another individual. Great leaders can change from the leader role to the follower role as the organization requires (Seteroff, 2006). For individuals to effectively lead an organization, their behaviors must be in alignment with present-day management expertise, advocating for change instead of solidarity, empowerment rather than dominance, teamwork or collaboration instead of competition, and diversity rather than conventionality. In spite of the fact that leaders and managers must regularly supervise orderliness, they cannot neglect the human aspect of organizations.

Employee satisfaction: Leaders' practices and behaviors affect employees' job satisfaction (Holdnak, Harsh, & Bushardt, 1993). Educational and business leaders consider the value of a more knowledgeable and new approach to leadership. Holdnak, Harsh, and Bushardt (1993) concluded that a transformational approach heightens employee involvement, proposing that a leader who practices a participatory leadership style positively influences followers' job contentment. Holdnak et al. (1993) also uncovered that dictatorial behavior reduces job contentment, indicating that leaders who incorporate dominance and control over subordinates will experience a reduction in employees' level of satisfaction and performance with work (Manning, 2015). Earlier researchers reached the same conclusion. The Creative Leadership Center in Greensboro, North Carolina, shed more light on the significance of leadership skills in their leadership study where 70% of frontline employees mentioned their biggest organizational problem was initiating adequate and satisfactory leadership strategy in all levels of organization (Bordieri, 1988; Vecchio, 1988). The center also looked at the characteristics of effective executives by studying 20 executives who had encountered disturbance in their profession or occupation. The ineffective leaders/managers were people that were supposed reign supreme, but were either terminated, given mandatory early retirement, or sustained in their current positions. The distinction linking the two sets of leaders was the manner in which they displayed their leadership potentials/skills (Bordieri, 1988).

Employee Productivity. Employees who are more engaged are more productive. Thus, an effective leader recognizes the significance of employees in attaining the objectives and goals of an organization, and understands that motivating and stimulating employees are of great significant in the attainment of these goals (Ojokuku et al., 2012). Therefore, successful organizations need effective leadership. Effective leaders enhance followers' talents and possibilities, and help followers achieve individual as well as organizational goals. The Hawthorne studies (Levitt & List, 2011) revealed that leadership style is a crucial employee success factor. Additionally, a leader's expectations can affect followers' work performance (Livingston, 2003). Jinyun, Chenwei, Yue, and Chia-huei (2016) also discussed the effects of self-fulfilling prophecy, the idea that a manager's expectations can influence employee results. The self-fulfilling prophecy states that managers who have high expectations of employees foster superior performance (Livingston, 2003). The self-fulfilling prophecy maintains the following: leaders have expectations of the individuals that answer to them; leaders intentionally or unintentionally convey these expectations and employees either consciously or unconsciously internalize or realize managers' expectations (Livingston, 2003). Employees' work performance mirrors manager expectations; that is, managers who communicate high expectations will receive good results, and managers who communicate low expectations will receive substandard results (Riley & Ungerleider, 2012).

Cultural considerations. Kirkman and Shapiro (2001) stated that leadership practices are related to the extent of follower job contentment, and job contentment could be dependent upon the level of individual value beliefs. Riley and Ungerleider (2012) revealed that an individual's cultural beliefs play a significant function in molding subordinate/worker response to characteristics of work, including leaders' responsibilities. Followers tend to react favorably to leaders who yield to behaviors that promote and encourage followers' cultural beliefs, and will respond inappropriately when leaders' behaviors do not support followers' individually held cultural beliefs (Kirkman & Shapiro, 2001). Therefore, to influence followers' positive behavior, leaders ought to be educated on ways individual cultural values and beliefs shape followers' responses to leadership style, and how followers' work environment behaviors and attitudes are impacted by the relationship between different styles of leadership and followers' cultural beliefs (Riley & Ungerleider, 2012).

Organizational effectiveness. Leadership is essential for organizational effectiveness, and "is the solution for group survival and a collective phenomenon" (Hogan & Kaiser, 2005, p. 172). An effective leadership plan resolves the problem of how to organize communal effort. "Leadership is an adaptive tool for individual and group survival that involves persuading people to set aside, for a time, their selfish pursuits and work in support of the communal interest" (Hogan & Kaiser, 2005, p. 172). Successful leaders are experienced in building relationships and acquiring status (Ojokuku, Odetayo, & Sajuyigbe, 2012). Good leaders are known by hard work, intelligence, and ambition (Hogan & Kaiser, 2005). Similarly, a leader's personality can significantly influence leadership style. Personality is a good predictor of bad and good leadership, "who we are, determines how we lead" (Hogan & Kaiser, 2005, p.175). Kirkman and Shapiro (2001) explained that personalities predict leadership effectiveness; thus, good leaders display modesty, humility, empathy, and compassion for others (Kirkman & Shapiro, 2001).

Recognizing and accepting the impact that leadership has on performance is essential since leadership is regarded by many to be the motivating force that improves organizations' productivity (Wren,

1995). Effective leadership is the beginning of management growth, which strengthens competitive edge and organizational performance improvement (Memoona, Kiran, & Bahaudin, 2015). Visionary leaders develop a strategic vision for a later date, disseminate that dream by framing and using metaphors, and demonstrate that dream by dramatizing and erecting commitment towards the dream (Memoona et al., 2015). Effective leadership brings unity, trust, dedication, inspiration, and increased performance in an organization. Frank, Eckrich, and Rohr (1997) examined the features that promote good standard in individuals who assist in the identification, prevention, or treatment of an illness; they discovered that good leadership plays an important role in the efficiency of the care transmittal system. It is assumed that preceptors or charge nurses are the brains behind excellent coordination and performances in transmitting good care and as such, should be sympathetic and have confidence in their subordinates (Frank, Eckrich, & Rohr, 1997). Morrison, Jones, and Fuller (1997) submitted that transformational and transactional leadership were favorably connected to job contentment, further corroborating Frank et al.'s findings.

Environmental influences. Brown (2011) explained that as environmental situations change, organizations must appropriately adapt if they are to remain competitive and successful because change brings about innovation; innovation absence leads to organizational failure. In today's global market that has witnessed constant evolution of technology, organizations fail because of their inability to adapt to technological changes, renewal, and a lack of vision (Brown, 2011). Therefore, the proper systems approach works with various arms of an organization, rather than in isolation to accomplish organizational goals. This enables managers/leaders to observe, analyze, and solve organizational problems whenever they arise.

Today's leaders are confronted with risky situations unlike those in the past; therefore, their ability to anticipate, cope, and or adapt risk-incurring environments makes them successful and their organizations more competitive (Brown, 2011). Reacting to change after the fact sets the organization up for failure. Therefore, any organization that exists in a changing business arena must have the capacity to adapt to change. For survival, organizations must develop methods of continuous self-renewal and should recognize when change is necessary, and should possess all that is needed to make appropriate and sustainable change (W. Gibb Dyer, Dyer, & Dyer, 2013).

Organizations must have flexibility and the capability for fast transformation to success in modern day business (Brown, 2011). The detection of issues and improvement areas within an organization is a key component in creating a high performing organization. Brown (2011) contended that all participants in an organization are required to hold some accountability, formulating a vision and enhancing the corporate culture. In any change program, an individual must recognize where he or she is positioned in the program before a course of action to reach desired goals may be mapped.

LEADERSHIP AND EMPLOYEE PERFORMANCE

Meyer, Srinivas, Lal, and Topolnytsky (2007) discovered a powerful connection between employees' job performance and leadership behavior. This quantitative correlational research study will further establish a connection between employee job satisfaction, innovation, leadership behavior, and organizational success. The same conclusion reached by Meyer et al. (2007) was also reached in 2014 by Sankey and Machin who examined a model of core proactive motivation processes for participation in non-mandatory professional development (PD) within a proactive motivation framework using the Self-Determination Theory perspective. Employees' active participation paved the way for more standard and potent allegiance to the organization as well as to the department publications on employee involvement show that involvement in matters affecting employee jobs heightens follower commitment, outcomes, and punctuality (Amah & Ahiauzu, 2013; Andries & Czarnitzki, 2014). Companies that encourage workers to take part in decision making are good at innovations and usually obtain the best from employees in terms of outcome, effectiveness, and dedication (Amah & Ahiauzu, 2013). Bhatti et al. (2011) discovered that employee participation and involvement brings about positive employee perceptions of the organization. Bhatti et al. (2011) also suggested that number and mix of applications are important issues in the involvement and dedication relationship.

While some researchers discovered that involvement is usually not required in gaining allegiance toward goals (Sankey & Machin, 2014), making subordinates involved in the planning could be a potent way of strengthening dedication with the organization (Andries & Czarnitzki, 2014). Involvement is essentially useful in expanding strategy toward goal executions. For these reasons, leaders must encourage employee inclusion in planning ways of realizing organizational goals (Bhatti et al., 2011). Involvement in an organization is powerful amongst subordinates who are included in decision making (Andries & Czarnitzki, 2014). The importance of employees' participation in matters that affect their work has been at the forefront of debate in among organizational scholars (Sankey & Machin, 2014). Including employees in expanding and executing organizational strategies can foster a sense of ownership, belonging, and self-esteem, and thus increase employee dedication to an organization. Moreover, employees' ideas, mastery, and experience can enhance the business plans and assure realistic and workable application (Amah & Ahiauzu, 2013).

Brown (2011) wrote about employee empowerment, stating that empowered employees are the difference makers in an organization concerning failure and success. Empowerment is a management practice that boosts employees' morale, giving power or authority to employees and or work group members to make decisions concerning their work, allowing them to take absolute responsibility for the outcome of such decisions (Huq, 2016). Empowerment is one of the organizational development intervention strategies that enhances the development and betterment of the individual members of the organization under the assumption that when an employee is more involved, efficient and skilled, the organization as a whole will improve (Brown, 2011). Employees who are empowered, develop a sense of responsibility and pride, and are more competent and proactive in assisting their organizations to actualize goals (Brown, 2011). Organizations meet excellence when they purposely move risk-taking and decision-making down to the least possible level (Huq, 2016).

Leaders should be open, clear in their expectations of followers, transparent, passionate, live by example, and be team players who can stand up for their team (Brown, 2011). Additionally, leaders must be firm and assertive in delivering their leadership roles, particularly when it comes to products, qualities, or services, and should not compromise. Once the team knows that their leaders have developed and established a clear path or vision, as well as decision criteria for them to live by, they will humbly follow the leader's guidance.

LEADERSHIP AND EMOTIONAL INTELLIGENCE

Emotional intelligence (EI) is a leadership competency that has attracted significant attention since the 1990s. Effective leaders possess strong EI (Goleman, 1998). Emotional intelligence is a kind of intelligence unassociated to functional or technical expertise. Leaders who exhibit EI have social skills that allow them to manage and inspire followers to achieve organizational goals. Most people are familiar with intelligent and skilled individuals who were upgraded into leadership positions because they excelled in their individual contributory roles, yet were unsuccessful in displaying sound leadership. Likewise, individuals with average intellectual capabilities have been upgraded to leadership positions and excelled. The distinction between these two sets of individuals is the level of their emotional intelligence (Goleman, 1998). Though technical skills and caliber of the intelligent quotient (IQ) are paramount, Goleman (1998) noted emotional intelligence as a vital ingredient of leadership. Additionally, "a person can have all the education in the universe, possess analytical skill, and an unending gift of brilliant ideas, but can still make a lousy leader due to lack of emotional intelligence" (Goleman, 1998, p. 94).

Studies of managerial derailment frequently connect low performance with low EI (Baah&Mekpor, 2017). Managers with low emotional intelligence are often involuntarily terminated, demoted, or their careers plateau below anticipated achievement levels. In many instances, derailment occurs due to an absence of self-awareness failure to adapt, and failure to manage relationships (Noe, 2012). These pro-social behaviors comprise emotional intelligence. To be successful in a leadership role, individuals must demonstrate technical and functional competence and emotional Intelligence. Goleman (1998) identified self-regulation, self-awareness, and empathy as three critical components of EI in the workplace.

Self-Regulation. Consider the following scenario: an employee presented inaccurate data to a customer and lost an important account. The individual's boss was angry and disappointed the employee lost the sale. In a situation like this, a leader has many behavioral options for expressing anger and disappointment. The leader can communicate concerns respectfully and appropriately or can publicly display hostile, aggressive behavior. Leaders who exhibit self-regulation select suitable emotional reactions. These leaders are able to keep cool under pressure. Self-regulation is an essential leadership quality. Baah and Mekpor (2017) believed the majority of the unpleasant things that take place in organizations are the by-product of impulsive behavior. People seldom intend to exaggerate profits, enlarge expense accounts, and misuse power for selfish gains. When an opportunity presents itself, people with low impulse control are vulnerable. Individuals who are capable of self-regulating are introverts and able to exhibit high frustration tolerance and negate impulsive urges. Although aggressive, short-tempered individuals are frequently viewed as "classic" leaders, their inability to self-regulate often creates difficulty for themselves and for others (Goleman, 1998).

Self-Awareness. The skill to carry out a truthful self-assessment is self-awareness (Romanowska, Larsson, & Theorell, 2014). Individuals who are conscious of themselves are knowledgeable of their weaknesses and strengths. Self-aware individuals are sincere not only with themselves, but also with others. Self-aware individuals also acknowledge the ramifications of their behavior on others and on their work. For example, a self-aware individual who clearly understands that putting off tasks can develop stress ensures that work is finished in a timely fashion (Romanowska et al., 2014). A self-aware person also understands that a personal standard may convey unreasonable expectations to others (Romanowska et al., 2014). Self-aware people are honest and can assess themselves realistically. Self-aware people can identify their strengths and weaknesses and can comfortably talk about them. They are non-defensive and can accept and apply constructive feedback. Leaders with high self-awareness are approachable and accepting of employee feedback. People with low self-awareness view constructive criticism as an attack or a symptom of failure, and employees are reluctant to approach these individuals (Goleman, 1998). Self-aware people are self-confident. They know their capabilities and their limitations and are unafraid to ask others for assistance (Romanowska et al., 2014). Self-aware people work to capitalize on their strengths and minimize their weaknesses. Although self-aware people are an asset in the workplace, Goleman (1998) indicated senior executives often do not consider the self-awareness competency when hiring future leaders.

Empathy. Empathy is the ability to "identify ourselves with someone and to feel what the other person is feeling" (Belzung, 2014, p. 178). To illustrate the concept of empathy, Goleman (1998) related how two leaders informed employees about a pending company merger. The first department manager held a meeting, announced the merger would create job duplication, and informed the group that many people would be fired. The second leader was honest about the situation, acknowledged and validated employees' fears, and committed to keeping people informed. The difference between how these leaders communicated with employees was empathy. The first leader did not consider what employees were feeling, whereas the second validated employees' concerns and acknowledged their fears. Empathy is an essential leadership trait for developing, enticing, and keeping top talent (Goleman, 1998).

Nonetheless, the manner by which leaders express their emotions plays a significant role in leader–follower relationship. Leaders' emotions affect the way followers think, act, and feel (Belzung, 2014). Leaders' can advertently or inadvertently show their emotions by vocal, facial, and other subliminal cues that can have a devastating impact on subordinates; thus, impact of leaders' emotional utterances on followers and performance has taken a center stage in most leadership articles and research (Romanowska et al., 2014). This research explored the effects leadership practices have on employees' performance for two reasons. First, the goal was to point out leadership practices that were proven by research to be detrimental to the survival of an organization; and second, the aim was to suggest those traits that enhance innovation, competitive advantage objectives, and employees' sense of belonging and self-worth in an organization. Simons, Leroy, Collewaert, and Masschelein (2015) and Skovholt, Gronning, and Kankaanranta (2014) demonstrated that leaders' positive emotional utterances usually bring pleasing results in terms of followers' performance and perceptions of leaders' effectiveness.

Similarly, Gooty, Connelly, Griffith, and Gupta (2010) suggested that leaders' negative emotional utterance is pessimistically linked to leader effectiveness, while Lindebaum and Fielden (2011) inferred that leaders' emotional utterances are linked to their followers' level of commitment, project progress, and performance. Nevertheless, whether leaders' negative emotional utterance leads to favorable follower performance needs more examination (Lindebaum & Fielden, 2011). The notion that negative emotional utterances are part and parcel of organizational life, survival, and that there exists a need for leaders to instill negative emotions to achieve organizational goals, to keep followers in check, and to get employees' cooperation has been advocated by many researchers. However, it is vitally important to spell out exactly when leadership negative emotional utterance heightens or decreases follower performance (Lindebaum & Fielden, 2010).

The leadership process only works if both leaders and followers are involved (P. Ruiz, Ruiz, & Martinez, 2011). Followers must be motivated to support the leader. Both leader and followers must have mutual trust (P. Ruiz et al., 2011). An ethical leader demonstrates good morals and empathy (P. Ruiz et al., 2011). Once a righteous leader is truly known and actions are demonstrated consistently, followers must have clear direction on where the team or organization is going (Lindebaum & Fielden, 2010). With little motivation and encouragement from their leaders, employees look to and marvel at competitors who are taking care of their employees with compassion (Lindebaum & Fielden, 2010).

Leaders must show empathy to encourage team members through the rough times and compliment them during successes (Sarros, Luca, Densten, & Santora, 2014). Individuals' leadership characteristics make them stand out. Managers tell people what to do. Leaders influence people to change (Holt & Marques, 2012). Aspiring leaders may not directly rescue employee out of a bad situation but could show compassion and empathy to the employee's plight. A visionary and trustworthy leader will plant a seed that causes a chain reaction to move toward the life an employee could have and things that matter most (Maxwell, 2013). The employee may begin to exhibit similar traits of empathy and compassion for others. The leader sits the tone and it becomes contagious throughout the organization as members follow this person and begin to change their environment and life's habits (Maxwell, 2013).

LEADERSHIP AND EMPLOYEE MOTIVATION

Motivation plays a significant role in any public or private organization. An organization whose leaders do not motivate their employees runs a risk of not achieving its goals. Employees' motivation is the avenue by which organizations inspire employees through rewards, incentives, and bonuses for achieving the organizations set goals. Motivation is the number one influential factor of human resources in an organization. Leaders should be motivating their followers for the best performance or for achieving the organizational goals. Motivation is the best instrument for best performance. Motivation leads to employees who take their responsibilities and duties seriously, and who perform to the best of their ability (Azar & Shafighi, 2013). Attractive salaries also play a significant role in increasing employee's output and performance in an organization (Muogbo, 2013). Assigning complicated tasks, providing excellent challenges, giving constructive feedback, and ensuring freedom from degrading evaluations are shown to facilitate intrinsic motivation (Charbonneau, Barling, & Kelloway, 2001). Preferences, opportunity for self-direction, and acceptance or admission of feelings are identified to increase intrinsic motivation of employees' as the constructs offer feelings of autonomy. Leaders can furnish followers with developmental feedback, participation in decision making, task completion information, and difficult or challenging task. Such actions will enhance employee intrinsic motivation through supportive monitoring, teaching, mentoring, participating, empowering, information sharing, knowledge co-creating, and inspiring behavior (Charbonneau et al., 2001). Moreover, intrinsic motivation is likely to thrive in ideas characterized by a sense of security and relatedness (Cho & Perry, 2011). Supportive monitoring and mentoring can help alleviate employees' fears and feelings of failures. Through encouraging risk-taking behaviors, leaders can unknowingly promote imagination and intellectual curiosity that be advantageous to the organization. Being aware of employees' needs, displaying or demonstrating empathy, appreciation and supporting individual followers' viewpoints and initiatives can enhance productivity and employees' performance (Cho & Perry, 2011).

Evaluation of data from current research studies on employee organizational loyalty and job satisfaction disclosed a positive correlation with transformational leadership style (Bowonder et al., 2010; Hickman, 2016; Kirkbride, 2006). Employees were more attentive and enthusiastic about being creative, innovative, and engaged in their work when leaders exhibit a transformational leadership style (Yang, 2012). Research suggested employee comfort; happiness, effectiveness of technology, leaders' emotional maturity; strategic skills and cognitive skills may influence organizational success (Thompson, 2014; Gharakhani et al., 2013; Aziz & Rizkallah, 2015; Mumford et al., 2017).

ORGANIZATIONAL SUCCESS

Success is measured by how well an organization is doing to attain its objective, vision, and goals (Thompson, 2014). Assessment of organizational success is a crucial aspect of tactical or prudent management. Success can emanate from an amalgamation of industry or environmental conditions, the tactic that decision makers choose, and the design in place to buttress the tactic (Thompson, 2014). Organizations vary in their prospective for profitability according to various factors overseeing their competitiveness, including the power of suppliers and buyers as well as the existence of obstacles to entry by potential competitors (Scott & Davis, 2007). CEOs or leaders of organizations ought to know how proficient their organizations are performing, and if they are not performing satisfactorily, be able to design better strategy for change. Success is a complicated concept; therefore, attention should be paid to how it is measured. To this end, Thompson (2014) initiated a new organizational theory from a sociological perspective which many scholars refer to as "contingency theory." Contingency theory somewhat stepped away from scientific and administrative theory that emphasized that there is no one best approach for leadership (Thompson, 2014). By distinction, Thompson posited that organizational situations such as, nature of the task, leader's persona, and makeup of the group determines the best suitable management technique. For example, the business as "usual" philosophy that led U.S auto makers to lose their market shares to Japanese automakers decades ago also compelled them to embrace the total quality management technique (TQM; Thompson, 2014). Thompson believed that organizational structures and dynamics should not be solely on goals and technology, but on coordination issues and situational uncertainties. In Thompson's view, companies should evaluate the effectiveness of technology from a sociological point of view.

MEASURES OF ORGANIZATIONAL SUCCESS

The wealth of instruments or devices by which to gauge organizational success can provide a different perspective about the organization's performance (Gharakhani, Farrokhi, & Farahamandian, 2013). Fortune 500 lists the largest U.S firms in terms of sales, even though those firms may not necessarily be the strongest performers in terms of growth or stock price (Gharakhani et al., 2013). While evaluating the correlation between TQM and success, scholars and business researchers have used various performance indicators like profit margin, customer loyalty, innovation, operational and quality performance, as well as balanced scorecard, each of which provide a popular framework to aid executives in understanding their organization's success (Thompson, 2014).

Nevertheless, most executives, measure performance by profit margin, growth, market share, customer satisfaction, and sales to better understand how well their organizations are performing in relation to their competition (Bigliardi & Galati, 2014). This study will employ innovation and job satisfaction to measure success, because it is believed that these two indicators are sufficient measures of an organization's health, and will provide reliable information (Cornelison, 2013). Scott and Davis (2007) posited that organizational success can be established by an organization's ability to utilize its resources to forecast its future. Many of today's organization perceive their employees as their greatest invaluable assets (Cornelison, 2013). According to Bon and Mustafa (2013), "for an organization to compete well and increase competitive advantage, they need to provide high-quality and innovative products and services" (p. 517). Bon and Mustafa suggested that TQM is of paramount importance in organizational success, particularly in-service industries. TQM and innovation aim at integrating organizational functions and objectives to satisfy customers and enlarge or expand competitive advantage (Bon & Mustafa, 2013). TQM is an all-inclusive philosophy where every employee is involved in organizational success, from the management process through the business process (Bon & Mustafa, 2013).

TQM and innovation provide sustainable development opportunities for increased success. The major communal goals of TQM and innovation are continuous improvement, fulfilling customer need, and an open culture (Bon & Mustafa, 2013). Cornelison (2013), Bon and Mustafa (2013), and Bigliardi and Galati (2014) were influenced by theorists such as Juran, Deming, Crosby, and Feigenbaum who contributed to the complex understanding of organizational success. Their studies also correlate with transformational leadership theory (Cornelison, 2013) that encourages collaboration, teamwork, constructive motivation, and intellectual stimulation, as it depends highly on information from management as well as workers to achieve goals.

The correlation between innovation and TQM dictates organizational performance and growth (Bon & Mustafa, 2013). TQM and innovation play an indispensable role in service business success, especially in creating and strengthening competitive edge, as well as having an immeasurable impact on customer satisfaction which is the goal of service organizations' business (Bon & Mustafa, 2013). The need for quality in the service industries has compelled and inspired many scholars to carry out studies on TQM practices and organizational effectiveness (Bon & Mustafa, 2013). TQM has been informed by fresh perspectives offered by organizational success scholarship (Bigliardi & Galati, 2014). Upgrading or enhancing the quality with which organizations convey products and services is pivotal for competing in an increasingly global marketplace (Gharakhani et al., 2013). TQM is accomplished through a combined effort of personnel at all departments and levels to widen or strengthen customer satisfaction by continuously upgrading and enhancing performance (Cornelison, 2013). TQM emphasizes procedure improvement, teamwork, supplier and customer involvement, training, and education to gain customer satisfaction, elimination of defects, and cost-effectiveness. TQM also produces the climate and culture vital for breakthroughs and technological advancement (Cornelison, 2013).

Therefore, TQM's fundamental assumption is that organizational members must collaborate with one another to accomplish quality that satisfies customers' needs. Gharakhani et al. (2013) explained that for TQM to be effective, all hands must be on deck. In essence, there must be an integration of teams because teams provide organizations with the ordered environment required for effectively and regularly implementing the TQM technique. The quality initiative should be instituted, and the continuous improvement procedure carried out by a well-organized team structure (Gharakhani et al., 2013). Many scholars have investigated the relationship between TQM and success. Gharakhani et al. (2013) and Cornelison (2013) maintained that proper implementation of TQM increases customers' satisfaction level and has a positive and significant effect on success. Gharakhani et al. (2013) indicated that gaining customer satisfaction is assumed to increase organizational profits by reducing costs through fewer returns and increasing revenues through customer loyalty (Bigliardi & Galati, 2014). Researchers employed various success indicators such as financial, innovative, quality and operational performance when investigating the correlation between TQM and success (Bigliardi & Galati, 2014; Gharakhani et al., 2013).

According to Gharakhani et al.:

> An essential part of assuring that TQM leads to sustained improvements in organizational profitability is that direct quantitative measures of manufacturing are used to assess the effectiveness of leaders' efforts to manage the development and implementation of TQM programs with the growing awareness that quality of final products and services is a strategic competitive variable (2013, p. 5).

Similarly, Bigliardi and Galati (2014) viewed TQM as a technique for continuous quality improvement whose sole objective is to meet and satisfy customers' needs. TQM utilizes special techniques to increase business and profits and enhance productivity by avoiding high cost, waste, rejects, reworks, and customer complaints. Some of TQM's benefits listed by Bigliardi and Galati (2014) include improved customer satisfaction, improved quality, orderliness in delivering products and services, and cost reduction. According to Bigliardi and Galati, the reason TQM has not received much attention in the R & D industries is due to the absence of R & D quality measurements, the absence of employee commitment, low tangibility, and repetition of R & D activities. To this end, Bigliardi and Galati suggested a four-phased model of implementation of TQM in the R & D industries that includes among other things, involvement, initiation, sustenance, and implementation.

The essential requirement for an effective implementation of TQM is the creation of an organizational culture where everybody at every phase of innovation and every management level clearly understand the importance of TQM and is committed to it (Bigliardi & Galati, 2014). Cornelison (2013) described TQM as a management technique to long-term success through customer satisfaction where every member of an organization take part in improving products, services, process, and the culture in which they work. It is a system that is focused on customer focus (Cornelison, 2013). Eight principle constraints that must be available within TQM practice are fact-based decision making, customer focused, process-centered, total employee participation, integrated system, systematic approach, communications, and continual improvement. The constraints are expected to work in unison to develop a system that will continuously improve all area of an organization leading to the ultimate goal of TQM which is "customer focus and improvement in customer satisfaction" (Cornelison, 2013, p.10).

INNOVATION AS A SUCCESS MEASURE

Organizations that refuse change and innovation are less likely to increase their market share and competitive ability and may ultimately be forced out of business because they lack innovative acumen (White & Bruton, 2011). Innovation ability is one of the major determinants of organizational survival and profitability (Mobbs, 2011). In today's ever-changing business arena, ideas that did not make sense many years ago are suddenly making sense, and ideas that made a great deal of sense yesterday do not make sense today (White & Bruton, 2011). This reality gives credence to why leaders must be visionary and innovative to adapt to ever changing world (White & Bruton, 2011). The success of any business depends primarily on making use of emerging or proven technologies and the ability to manage, utilize, or harness those emerging or proven technologies (Tidd & Bessant, 2013). Chadwick (2016) submitted that one of the reasons organizations do not innovate is that leaders have failed to recognize the importance of their role in the innovation process. Thus, in determining the capability of a company to handle technology and innovation, it is essential for managers and leaders to have a solid understanding of the company's capabilities (White & Bruton, 2011).

White and Bruton (2011) submitted that capabilities are the set of organizational factors that support and facilitate an organization's strategies. They are the engine blocks for the company's plans that include abilities and skills. Therefore, it is imperative that organizations perform an in-depth analysis of various features of their current innovation capabilities, processes and procedures, evaluating key measures, and establishing weaknesses and strengths (Mobbs, 2011). Corporate executives need to periodically audit organization's technology and innovation capability so as to get a real picture of the overall performance of the organization, the innovation process, and where that process needs improvement (Tidd & Bessant, 2013). The periodic audit is an authentic means of enhancing innovation throughout the organization (Mobbs, 2011).

Managing technology and innovation is important in a society where increasing sophistication of consumers and the rapid pace of technological development have reduced product life cycles (White & Bruton, 2011). For this reason, there is a need for organizations to be more dynamic in managing technology and innovation (White & Bruton, 2011). Similarly, the increasing global competition means that organizations need to elevate or maximize competitiveness through effective utilization of new technologies, because as technology changes, the tools of management must change as well (Tidd & Bessant, 2013). Though innovation is an embodiment of change, it is linked with a high degree of risk because the result of R&D is usually unpredictable; only 12% to 20% of R&D projects result in products that make it to end-users; the rest are failures (Jones, 2013). In as much as innovation can bring about new technologies and products, it can also bring changes that organizations do not want, such as inefficient technologies and products for which there is no consumer need. These technological changes can be an opportunity as well as a threat, destructive even though creative (Jones, 2013). They help in creating new product innovations that organizations can take advantage of, and at the same time, can lessen or destroy the demand for the products made by less innovative and unknown companies (Jones, 2013).

EMPLOYEE JOB SATISFACTION AS A SUCCESS MEASURE

From time immemorial, the subject of employee satisfaction has magnetized extensive empirical investigation, giving rise to many definitions. Locke and Lathan (1976) defined employee satisfaction as an enjoyable, gratifying, or positive state of mind derived from the evaluation of one's job experiences. Islam, Rasul, and Ullah (2012) defined job satisfaction as an emotional reaction to a job situation, a crucial factor for a company's success. Job satisfaction is an outcome of workers' impression on how satisfactorily their job can meet or exceed their expectations (Amissah, Gamor, Deri, & Amissah, 2016). Job satisfaction can be attained when an employee performs to the best of the employee's ability or feels appreciated and part of the organization (Islam et al., 2012). Performance and Job satisfaction are positively influenced by rewards.

Job satisfaction delineates how pleased and contented an employee is with his or her job (Islam et al., 2012). The more satisfied employees are with the job, the more committed and dedicated they are likely to be in discharging duties. Islam et al. (2012) identified various factors that can influence job satisfaction. They include the need for management to construct a condition that fosters employee participation, job enlargement, job rotation designed to reduce boredom and repetitiveness, job enrichment, involvement of employees in the decision-making process, constructive feedback, employee empowerment, which is giving power or authority to employees and or work group members to make decisions concerning their work, and taking absolute responsibility for the outcome of such decisions (Amissah et al., 2016). It is one of the organization development (OD) intervention strategies that enhances the development and betterment of the individual members of the organization under the assumption that when an employee is more involved, efficient, and skilled, the organization as a whole will improve (Brown, 2011).

Rewards and recognition enhance job satisfaction. Effective leaders usually recognize, appreciate, and reward employees' hard work. Rewarding employees not only boosts trust but deepens and strengthens allegiance. Leaders can reward by praise, publicly recognizing employees, giving paid vacations, providing free days, taking employees out for lunch, implementing extended lunch time, or sending employees personal emails thanking them for a job well done (Cho & Perry, 2011).

VARIABLES THAT AFFECT ORGANIZATIONAL SUCCESS

Factors such as organizational culture, climate, and training, can influence organizational performance, but recent technological advancement has opened a new era for different global competition (Aziz & Rizkallah, 2015). Conventional organizational management is no longer regarded suitable strategy in this ever-changing, ruthlessly competitive global market (Ho, 2008). Advancements in technology have given way to other factors such innovation, moral principle, emotional maturity, self-confidence, energy and stress tolerance, knowledge, and experience are some of the proven qualities that are part of being a successful and efficient leader (Yukl, 2013). Leaders often fail due to a lack of or weak interpersonal attributes such as technical, administrative, cognitive, or strategic skills that are essential for leadership effectiveness and advancement, and an inability to handle pressure (Yukl, 2013). Thus, organizational success requires the collective effort of leaders and subordinates (Yukl, 2013).

ADMINISTRATIVE SKILLS

Administrative skills are those skills leaders use to manage an organization, skill such as mentorship, commitment, willingness, and altruism to share mistakes and lessons learned with others (Buckley & Curd, 2012). It is clear that many leadership and administrative skills are not innate, but learned, acquired learned behaviors that can make or break a leader (Buckley & Curd, 2012). According to Buckley and Curd (2012), psychiatric associations and societies have been investing in leadership development by sponsoring fellowships that foster, promote, develop, and complement leadership skills. Buckley and Curd (2012) referenced Association of Chairs of Departments of Psychiatry (AACDP) who in direct response to the growing need to groom leaders for success launched a fellowship for senior psychiatrists that demonstrated an interest in becoming an academic chair. Good administrative skills help leaders carry out the missions and goals of an organization and build relationships with followers to efficiently accomplish the tasks at hand (Sultana, 2012).

NON-TECHNICAL SKILLS (NTS)

Success has often been attributed to non-technical skill and leaders fail due to lack of NTS (Yukl, 2013). Non-technical skills (NTS) are not cognitive skills, such as planning, decision-making, and conscious knowledge of the immediate environment or social expertise such as communication and teamwork that can have significant impact to the successful accomplishment of a determined task or tasks (Scott, Revera, McRitchie, Riviello, Smink, & Yule, 2016; Hjortdahl, Ringen, Naess, & Wisborg, 2009). Scott et al. (2016) submitted that 50 to 80% of errors or adverse events across many high-risk professions such as medicine and leadership are due to human behavior related to nontechnical skill. According to Hjortdahl et al. (2009), Non-technical skills give leaders confidence and a base to discharge their duties without fear, and as a leader, it is essential to know how to do everything and most importantly how to delegate things you cannot do. Leaders with high technical competence make team members confident and non-technically skilled leaders often "doubt whether or not they had the professional expertise required for the given situation" (Hjortdahl et al., 2009, p. 4)

COGNITIVE SKILLS

Mumford, Todd, Higgs, and McIntosh (2017) study on cognitive skills and leadership performance revealed that intelligence is positively related to leader emergence and performance. Mumford et al. (2017) submitted that the effects of cognitive abilities on leadership performance are central to expertise and Intelligence that ultimately defines the speed and depth of information processing when working on complex problems. Leaders who are skilled at forecasting is less likely to conclude or accept that plans will work without emanation of significant problems, lack of confidence, contingency planning, and other negative consequences (disrespect, dishonor, etc.,) it brings, will compel and encourage creative thought on the part of leaders (Mumford et al., 2017). Knowledge of potential flaws or ambiguities in plans emanating from predictions may account for the lack of trust or credence exhibited by some of the best leaders (Mumford et al., 2017). At the same token, recognition of those flaws may serve as a positive stimulus for creative thinking for leaders. Therefore, cognitive skills along with strategic skills are needed by leaders (Mumford et al., 2017).

SUMMARY OF LITERATURE REVIEW

Effective leadership styles have a significant impact on organizational success (Hogan & Kaiser, 2005). Evidence shows a relationship exists between leaders' emotional intelligence, self-regulation, self-awareness, empathy, motivation, intellectual stimulation, reward, employee satisfaction, innovation, job satisfaction, and organizational success (Bass, 1990; Kirkbride, 2006). Leaders' practices and behaviors as well as employees' perception of leader practices and behaviors have an impact on employee performance, job contentment, and effectiveness.

The literature review encompassed a dialogue of the impact of leadership styles on organizational success. Leaders must continually evaluate personal skills and traits that indicate leader effectiveness. Skills, behaviors, and leadership styles are the best predictors of success in a managerial profession and occupation. Thus, qualities such as moral principle, emotional maturity, self-confidence, energy and stress tolerance, knowledge, and experience are some of the proven qualities that are part of being a successful and efficient leader (Yukl, 2013). Leaders often fail due to a lack of or weak interpersonal attributes such as technical, administrative, cognitive, or strategic skills that are essential for leadership effectiveness and advancement, and an inability to handle pressure (Yukl, 2013). Thus, organizational success requires the collective effort of leaders and subordinates (Yukl, 2013). The review also covered relevant leadership theories such as the transformational, transactional, laissez-faire, the contingency approach, Theory X & Y, behavioral approach, path-goal theory, the trait approach, and measures of organizational success as well as some of the factors that could positively and negatively influence organizational success.

The review of the literature confirmed that previous researchers had not examined the relationships between leadership styles (i.e., transformational, transactional, and laissez-faire) and organizational success measured by innovation and job satisfaction. Researchers had not investigated whether transformational, transactional, and laissez-faire leadership styles are significantly related to a firm's innovation and employee job satisfaction. This research seeks to fill that information gap. Chapter 3 contains a discussion of the selected research methodology and suitability of the design. The chapter includes instrumentation, sampling, population, methods, data collection technique(s), and instrument reliability and validity.

CONCLUSION

There are many approaches to Leadership. Leadership style is an integral part of organizational success (Bowonder, Dambal, Kumar, & Shirodkar, 2010). An exhaustive review of the literature disclosed significant correlations between transformational leadership style of leaders and employee attitude and job performance both at the team, individual, and organizational levels (Avolio & Bass 2004; Bas, 1999). It has been established by many studies that transformational leadership is a good predictor of employee loyalty, commitment, or allegiance in varied organizational setting (Eisenbeiss et al., 2008; Barling et al., 1996r, Howell & Avolio, 1993). Many of literature integrates correlational research studies as well as field experiment (Bass, 1999, Barling et al., 1996) and studies that employed nonexperimental designs, such as a cross-sectional survey (Leach, 2005), a correlational design (Emery & Barker, 2007).

Multiple regression analysis techniques were principally used in many current and germinal sources of the literature to assess relationships/ correlation between leadership style and organizational success (Barling et al., 1996; Walumbwa et al., 2005; Emery & Barker, 2007). In spite of the fact that a correlational research design does not permit the establishment of causal relationships, literature sources furnished proof concerning statistical relationships between transformational leadership style and employee job satisfaction, innovation, retention, empowerment, and job performance in diverse organizational settings (Bono & Judge, 2004; Walumbwa et al., 2005; Frooman et al., 2012).

The review of the literature confirmed that previous researchers had not evaluated the relationships between leadership styles (i.e., transformational, transactional, and laissez-faire) and organizational success measured by innovation and job satisfaction. Researchers had not investigated whether transformational, transactional, and laissez-faire leadership styles are significantly related to a firm's innovation and employee job satisfaction. Assessing the level and the direction of the relationship between transformational, transactional, and laissez-faire leadership style of managers of companies that have been in business for more than 10 years can help address this known gap.

CHAPTER 3

METHODOLOGY

The purpose of this quantitative correlational study was to investigate if a correlation exists between leadership style, innovation and job satisfaction as indicators of organizational success in companies that have been in business for more than 10 years. The study also ascertained if there exists a particular leadership style employed by leaders of XYZ retail industry organizations that have been in business for more than 10 years by encouraging and promoting innovation while other companies in the same retail industry have failed. In this chapter, the author discussed the chosen research methodology and suitability of the design as well as the operational variables, demographic variables, how variables were measured and the level of measurement, and implications for the selection of inferential statistics technique. The chapter also addressed the descriptive statistics for each variable and rationale, participants' informed consent, confidentiality, sampling methods, population, data collection technique(s), instrumentation, instrument reliability, and validity as well as the summary.

RESEARCH DESIGN

A descriptive quantitative correlational research design method was employed to actualize the study purpose and address the problem. The justification for the use of descriptive research was to illustrate the current event, incident, or situation using numbers or words (Neuman,

2011). Because of its inability to examine relationships and to determine the strength of variables under investigation, a qualitative method was not an appropriate investigatory tool for this study (Keith, 2015). In a descriptive correlational study, investigators create comprehensive records and scrutinize many subjects, but cannot make predictions or determine causality; they solely describe the participants and behaviors (Leedy & Ormrod, 2013). Correlational studies delineate a particular situation or event in a manner that transmits or conveys the picture of what is being investigated (Neuman, 2011). The descriptive quantitative correlational method was also suitable because the variables of interest were measured using questionnaires containing Likert-type scales (Meyers, Gamst, & Guarino, 2013).This approach helped in deciding if there is a correlation between leadership style and company success as measured by innovation and job satisfaction, and if there is a particular leadership style employed by leaders of XYZ organization that have been in business for more than 10 years. Transformational leadership style, transactional leadership style, and laissez-faire leadership styles form the independent variables, while organizational success, as described by innovation and employee job satisfaction, served as the criterion variables.

The behavior dimensions of the three leadership styles were obtained through close-ended questions to the respondents. The Multifactor Leadership Questionnaire (MLQ-5x; Avolio & Bass, 2004) was used to evaluate the leadership styles of transformational, transactional, laissez-faire, and job satisfaction, while the Statistics Canada's Survey of Innovation and Business Strategy (SIBS) was used to measure innovation. Numerous researchers have attested the potency of the Multifactor Leadership Questionnaire (Avolio & Bass, 2004; Gillespie & Mann, 2004). The MLQ model has undergone series of upgrades to mitigate whatever imperfections it might have; Form 5X is one such upgrade (Avolio & Bass, 2004). Avolio and Bass's (2004) version of the MLQ model is a multicultural tool for capturing a wider spectrum of leadership behaviors, while at the same time isolating or separating effective from ineffective leaders. Independent reviews of the SIBS academics and business leaders throughout Canada described SIBS as an apt instrument using psychometric properties (Statistics Canada Catalogue, 2009).

Based on the literature review, the two research questions reflect the purpose statement of the study.

RQ1. What is the relationship between leadership style and job satisfaction in companies that have been in business for more than 10 years?

RQ2. What is the relationship between leadership style and innovation in companies that have been in business for more than 10 years?

Research questions provide direction on the type of data to be collected and how such data may be analyzed and interpreted (Curtis, Comiskey, & Dempsey, 2016; Leedy & Ormrod, 2013). Farrugia et al. (2010) maintained that the development of a research question and a supportive hypothesis is an essential step, and that a precise research question drives the investigation and the implementation of the study. The variables, survey instrument, and number of questions for each variable used to generate data for the research questions are outlined in Table 6.

STUDY HYPOTHESES AND VARIABLES

The following hypotheses were prompted by the research question and are essential to non-experimental research (Leedy & Ormrod, 2013). The hypotheses are intelligent, educated assumptions on how the research problem might be solved.

$H1_a$: Leadership style will be positively associated with job satisfaction in companies that have been in business for more than 10 years.

$H1_0$: Leadership style will not be positively associated with job satisfaction in companies that have been in business for more than 10 years.

$H2_a$: Leadership style will be positively associated with innovation in companies that have been in business for more than 10 years.

$H2_0$: Leadership style will not be positively associated with innovation in companies that have been in business for more than 10 years.

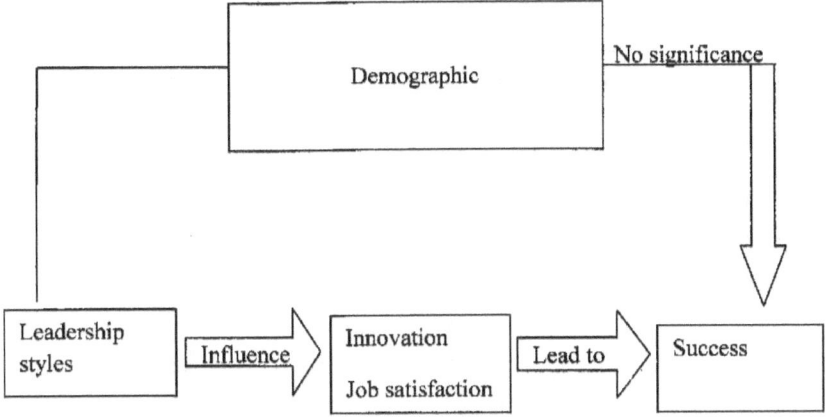

Figure 5: Hypotheses and variables operational model

Figure 5: Hypotheses and variables operational model

VARIABLES

Variables are essential in any study because they guide and drive the research process and enables researchers to pursue their studies with enthusiasm and maximum curiosity (Flannelly, 2014). Variables are used in constructing conceptual frameworks and in analyzing statistical data gathered for the study, especially in quantitative studies (Flannelly, 2014). Variables are constructs that are different or are expected to change among groups in a study. The dependent variable is subject to change depending on the outcome of an experimental manipulation of the predictor variable or variables (USC Libraries Research Guides, 2017). Independent variables (predictors) are variables that can be manipulated and dependent variables (criterion) are those variables that cannot be manipulated (Greenland et al., 2014).

Therefore, in this quantitative correlational research study, the variables that guided the study are the leadership styles, innovation, job satisfaction, and organizational success (Table 1). Leadership style was the predictor (independent variables), while organizational success, as described by innovation and employee job satisfaction was the criterion (dependent variable).

Demographic variables. Demographic variables cannot be manipulated and are used to delineate study samples and establish if samples are representative of the population of interest (Kaur, 2013). The demographic variables for this study are: gender, age, education level, and position occupied in the company (lower level, middle-level, upper-level management).

How variables were measured: The MLQ-5x (Avolio & Bass, 2004) was employed to evaluate the leadership styles of the participating leaders, while the SIBS was used to identify innovation. The MLQ-5x was chosen due to its efficacy in past investigations on leadership (Gillespie & Mann, 2004). The SIBS was selected because it is a varied tool for assessing innovation (Statistics Canada Catalogue, 2009). Leadership styles (transformational, transactional, and laissez-faire) are predictor variables and were measured based on leaders' style of leadership, perception, attitude, emotional intelligence, or behavior, contingent reward, management-by-exception (active) and management-by-exception (passive) as well as show little or no concern in how and when tasks are completed gives little input and anticipates little in return, scales for measuring leadership style. The individual questions on the MLQ were initially measured on a 0-5 Likert scale, which is ordinal in nature. However, the results from this scale were transformed into a mean score for each subscale and used as the mean of different sets of individual questions (Flannelly, 2014). Similar studies the researcher used as foundations for the literature review such as Hodlnak, Harsh, and Bushardt (1993) paper, Bordieri's (1988) research, Vecchio's study (1988) used parametric analyses such as regressions, Pearson correlations, or t tests. Across these papers, most assumed that the subscales (transformational, transactional, LF, etc.) should be treated as continuous, this was corroborated by Johnson and Creech (1983), Zumbo and Zimmerman (1993), and more recently, de Winter and Dodou (2012). Though Likert scales are clearly ordinal in theory, research has shown that when there are 5 or more categories, there is relatively little harm in using parametric analyses with them (Johnson & Creech, 1983; Zumbo & Zimmerman, 1993). Some researchers also use these parametric statistics when there are 4 ordinal categories, although this may be problematic at times. However, these studies describe the use of individual questions, particularly as dependent variables, and do not reflect what was used in this research. For cases such as the calculation of subscales as a result of means from several items, which is the procedure used to score the MLQ, the research is more clear.

When two or more Likert or ordinal items are combined, the number of possible values for the composite variable increases beyond 5 categories (i.e., the sum and subsequent mean of two items has a total of 10 possible values; the sum and subsequent mean of three items has a total of 15 possible values, etc.). Thus, it is a usual practice to treat these composite scores as continuous variables. This continues across more and more categories, bringing the total number of possible values up by an additional 5 with each new item averaged into a scale. However, de Winter and Dodou (2012) took this a step further to figure out whether this common practice was a valid way of deciding between parametric and nonparametric tests. When comparing the results of parametric or non-parametric tests, de Winter and Dodou found similar error rates in terms of Type I and Type II error regardless of whether a parametric or nonparametric approach was used for variables with this many possible values. Beyond this point, Type I errors were similar for both parametric and non-parametric tests even when conducted on five-point Likert scale individual items (de Winter & Dodou, 2010). More recently, Sullivan and Artino (2013) found similar results.

Each question was ranked and average scores for items on each scale were calculated. The acquired transformational leadership scores were added and divided by the number of transformational subscales to obtain an average score for transformational leadership style. The transactional leadership scores were added and divided by the number of transactional subscales to get an average score for transactional leadership style, the same thing was done for laissez-faire leadership style, innovation and job satisfaction for each respondent.

Implications for the selection of inferential statistical technique: Inferential statistics was selected because participants were selected at random and inferences were made from the study data to reach conclusions that extended beyond the study data. It was used to test the hypotheses to reach a conclusion as to whether the difference is statistically insignificant or statistically significant (Gupta, 2012).

Descriptive statistics for each variable and the rationale: The study employed graphical representation such as bar chart, line graph, circle graph/chart, frequency distribution, central tendency, scatter plot, and histogram whenever necessary. Greenland et al. (2014) explained that descriptive statistics is the instrument used by researchers to communicate the meaning of data sets in a way that makes them easy for the readers to understand. In essence, descriptive statistics is a summary of sets of research data. Data were broken down into graphic representation, frequency distribution, variability, central tendency, and relations among variables. The use of each of the descriptive statistics enhanced the validity of data, communicated more meaning, believability, and most importantly, provided a concise summary of the data (Hairs, Black, Babin, & Anderson, 2010).

INFORMED CONSENT

An e-mail was sent to the participants prior to the survey, outlining the research purpose, participant time obligation, and the significance of the study to the organization. Included in the informed consent e-mail was information on estimated time, age requirement, withdrawal procedures, and possible risks if any, for participating in the research study, and an instruction on how to complete both the MLQ and the SIBS. Participants were assured of the confidentiality of their responses, and of their right to refuse or terminate participation at any time. Participation in the research study was optional, and completing the survey was anonymous with no retention of Internet protocol addresses or any information associating participants with specific survey responses. A link with an "Agree" or "Disagree" button was provided for participants to acknowledge or decline their consent to participate. Participants were told that clicking the "Agree" button means that the participant has read and understood the content of the informed consent and has accepted to participate. By clicking "Agree" the participant automatically has access to the survey instruments; clicking "Disagree" denied access to the survey instruments.

CONFIDENTIALITY

Participants were assured of the confidentiality of their responses to the MLQ and the SIBS by completing the electronic consent letter (Appendix A) and informed consent form (Appendix B) in the host website (Mind Garden and Survey Monkey) before completing the survey instruments. The investigator is to retain all electronically stored research documentation for three years; after that period, all files and databases holding results will be deleted. The Web-based survey administrator, Mind Garden and Survey Monkey, hosted the survey instruments respectively and collected survey responses from respondents. Each host maintains a strict privacy policy that ensured the privacy and confidentiality of data, thus, limiting access to the survey instruments and related tools for the investigator via a login process. The investigator is the sole owner of the survey instrument as well as data collected from the survey.

SAMPLING METHODS

Through careful sample selection, the probability of introducing new and unwanted variables into the study was reduced. Thus, this correlational study made use of random probability sampling method where members of the population had an equal probability of being chosen (Flannelly, 2014). Boni, Silva, Bastos, Pechansky, and Vasconcellos (2012) explained that selecting subjects randomly can increase the likelihood of the sample representing the population as a whole. Stratified samplings were also explored because of the heterogeneity and demography of the population. Greenland et al. (2014) posited that a 5% sampling error and 95% percent confidence level is significant and acceptable. The effect size, the power of the statistical test, and the number of parameters to estimate is most important criteria for selection of a research sample for hypotheses testing (Thietart & Wauchope, 2001). Since the population of the study was somewhat small, Soper (2015) statistical calculators was used to calculate the sample size. From the population of 122 members of two small retail companies, the minimum sample size of 76 individuals was obtained.

Anticipated effect size (F^{2}):	0.15
Desired statistical power level:	0.8
Number of predictors:	3
Probability level:	0.05

Minimum required sample size: 76

Questionnaires were emailed to the participants with step-by-step information on how to complete the questionnaires. One hundred twenty-two (122) copies of the questionnaire and SIBS were dispersed, and all 122 copies were expected to be returned completed. The reason behind the 100% anticipated return was because of the purpose and benefit of the study.

POPULATION

The population of interest for this study was human resource personnel and managers aged 25-65 years from the XYZ retail company. These individuals of interest comprised the target population which set the boundary for the study. The population consisted of men and women who have been in their current leadership positions for more than five years. The researcher had access to the XYZ Company's electronic directory from where the names were generated; the questionnaire was sent to potential participants via email. This was in keeping with the companies' policies that forbid face-to-face meetings in their places of business as permission to meet in the company premises was not granted.

DATA COLLECTION PROCEDURES

Data collection is an essential feature of empirical investigation. Imprecise data collection can have a devastating impact on the outcome of a study (Greenland et al., 2014). Ponto (2015) explained that data may be collected through questionnaires, tests, focus groups, interviews, observations, and secondary or existing data. This study utilized questionnaires that were assigned numerical values through Likert-type scales. The questionnaire was sent to respondents by e-mail and was closed-ended. The questionnaire assessed participants' perceptions and opinions and supplied self-reported demographic information (Greenland et al., 2014). The questionnaires consisted mainly multiple-choice questions. Feedback from the questionnaires were plated and transmuted into quantitative data to facilitate demarcation of the data responses into reliant and non-reliant variables.

Data for this study came from the employees of the two XYZ retail companies in the metropolitan Detroit area that granted the researcher permission to survey. The Participants of the study were recruited via email after getting permission from the firms' president and or owners to solicit for participation from their employees. The data collection process commenced after the University of Phoenix Institutional Review Board granted permission to carry out the study. The method of selecting research participants was random probability sampling where members of the population had an equal probability of being chosen.

Data collection commenced on July 28, 2018 and was completed on August 26, 2018. On July 10, 2018, each potential participant received an introductory letter, an invitation to participate in the research which included a description of the purpose of the study and assurance of the protection of the identity and confidentiality of their responses to the survey questions. Five days letter, July 15, 2018, the informed consent form was administered online. The people who choose to participate in research were instructed to read the informed consent document and check the "Agree" box indicating their voluntary and willingness to take part in the study. On July 28, 2018, a link to MindGarden and SurveyMonkey was made available to the participants who signed the informed consent granting them access to the survey questionnaires. The completion of the surveys took 15 minutes and 2 minutes respectively for most respondents.

The survey was accessible to the participants for almost one month. One week before the end of data collection period and as the number of completed surveys slowly increased, the minimum sample had not been reached, a follow-up email was sent to those who have not responded to the surveys, reminding them of the closing date. There were 45 items from the Multifactor Leadership Questionnaire (MLQ) (Bass & Avolio, 1995) and 12 items from the Statistics of Canada's Survey of Innovation and Business Strategy (SIBS).

The MLQ instrument contained five subscales, inspirational motivation, idealized influence (attributed/behavioral), individualized consideration, and intellectual stimulation, to measure transformational leadership style and three subscales, management-by-exception (active &passive) and contingent reward, to assess transactional leadership style (Avolio & Bass, 1995). Transactional leadership style, transformational leadership style, and laissez-faire leadership were the predictor variables while employee innovation and job satisfaction were criterion variables in the study. The SIBS was the instrument for employee innovation.

INSTRUMENTATION

Measurement must be reliable and valid (Greenland et al., 2014). Any research that fails to live up to this expectation should not be trusted. An instrument is said to be reliable if the results are consistent, and valid if it measures what it was meant to measure (Greenland et al., 2014). This correlational study used the SIBS, an instrument used in measuring innovation. The MLQ was employed as the standard instrument for assessing transformational and transactional leadership behavior and job satisfaction (Avolio & Bass, 2004; Bass & Avolio, 2000). According to Rowold (2005), the MLQ-5x gives an in-depth synopsis of how often leaders are viewed displaying particular behaviors along a full range of leadership performance.

Table 3
Organizational Success Survey Instrument Alignment

Instrument	Independent Variables:		
MLQ	**Transformational**	**Transactional**	**Laissez- faire**
	Q16, Q18, Q37	Q4. Q11. Q12.	Q10, Q15, Q12,
	Q1, Q2, Q8, Q9	Q8, Q14, Q17	Q13, Q20, Q28
	Dependent Variable:	**Employee**	**Employees**
		Innovation	**Job Satisfaction**

MLQ	Q27, Q32, Q18	Q 45, Q3	Q31, Q34, Q38, Q41, Q40, Q42, Q44
		Q4, Q5, Q7	
Self-Efficacy	Q29, Q33, Q35,	Q36, Q39, Q20	

INSTRUMENT RELIABILITY AND VALIDITY

Many studies have confirmed the efficacy of the MLQ-5x (Gillespie & Mann, 2004). According to Avolio and Bass (2004), many industries including government parastatals and non-governmental agencies, fortune 500 companies, the military, and so many sectors of small businesses has been using MLQ for more than 20 years. Furthermore, MLQ is a multicultural instrument, various forms of MLQ has been administered in over 35 countries of the world and in many languages (Rowold, 2005; Avolio & Bass, 2004). The effectiveness of the MLQ over time reinforces the trustworthiness, reliability, and the validity of the instrument. The Multifactor Leadership Questionnaire Manual discloses accounts of the validity and reliabilities of the MLQ 5-x survey. The comprehensive study by Rowold (2005) and Avolio and Bass (2004) to reevaluate features of leadership (i.e., transactional and transformational) utilizing the MLQ 5x involved foreign organizations as well as the United States. The reliabilities for all leadership factor scales and for items ranged from 0.74 to 0.94 (Avolio & Bass, 2004). The SIBS is comprehensive and requires employees (participants) to furnish information on the number of new or improved products, marketing innovation, and the percentage of expenses allocated toward innovation (Statistics Canada Catalogue, 2009)

DATA ANALYSIS PROCEDURES

The collected data was analyzed using IBM® SPSS® Statistical Analysis Program Version 24 (IBM, 2016). The use of statistics reveals the kind of relationships that exist among variables, disclosing patterns and trends, and allowing researchers to compare the average between the groups in a study to determine whether the means are statistically significantly incompatible to each other (Greenland, Senn, Rothman, Carlin, Poole, Goodman, & Altman, 2016). Statistics test the null hypothesis (Greenland et al., 2016).

Upon securing the required number of completed surveys, data from sections corresponding to demographic information, leadership style, employee innovation and employee job satisfaction were coded, transferred into the SPSS and verified. Average scores for each predictor and criterion variables were computed. Preliminary analyses were performed to check the data for the assumptions of multiple regression analysis for hypotheses testing. The reliability of measures was computed for each predictor and criterion variable. Checking for missing data was not necessary because the surveys designed using Survey Monkey and MindGarden platform disqualified or expelled a possibility that respondents leave out responses. The program made it mandatory for participants to answer each question in a section before going on to the next section of the survey. Descriptive and interferential statistical analyses of research data were completed using IBM ® SPSS® version 24(IBM, 2016) program.

A correlational design was used to assess the relationship between the variables and test the research hypotheses (Flannelly, 2014). A correlational was the appropriate analysis according to Hair et al. (2010) correlational should be explored if the aim of research is to establish the relationship between two or more dependent variables. Thus, a Pearson correlation which evaluates the linear relationship between two continuous variables was used. Pearson, according to Laerd Statistics (2018) is a parametric test that attempts to draw a line of best fit through the data of two variables; it indicates how well the data points to the line of best fit. The advantages of using a parametric test are that it has more statistical power, in other words, a parametric test is more able to lead to a rejection of H0. Pearson correlation and parametric testing are preferred because they provide estimates and confidence intervals and can be generalized to more complex analyses (Altman & Bland, 2009).

Descriptive statistics. In the study, research variables were assessed using ordinal scale. Likert-scales of psychometric tests developed to produce equal interval data (Black, 1999) was used to assess transformational, transactional, laissez-faire leadership style, which represent the predictor variables as well as job satisfaction, and companies' success, which represent the criterion variables. The descriptive statistics that encompasses measures of validity and central tendency was employed to describe the leadership styles (predictor variables) and innovation, job satisfaction, and companies' success (criterion variables). The measures of central tendency (standard deviation, mean, mode, median, and range) were calculated for these continuous interval variables (Flannelly, 2014). Ordinal scale was used to measure demographic variables, which in this study are: age, education level, gender, and position occupied. A frequency distribution was computed for each value of demographic data to outline and delineate the research sample using percentages (Flannelly, 2014).

Inferential statistics. The option of a statistical analysis method in the study was influenced by the research questions and the research variables (Flannelly, 2014). Since the dependent variable job satisfaction was measured as a continuous variable, a Pearson correlation was more appropriate than a Spearman correlation. The inferential statistics was utilized to test the hypotheses and make judgments on the population based on the understanding about the sample (Frankfort-Nachmias & Leon-Guerrero, 2006). Statistical assessment and hypotheses testing were interdependent and provided the basis for assessing statistical cogency of research (Black, 1999). The goal of inferential statistics is to describe how likely a result is to be in consideration of the sampling error (Frankfort-Nachmias & Leon-Guerrero, 2006). A correlational procedure was carried out to test the relatedness of the variation in each criterion variable which might be ascribed to the regression of predictor variables by computing the F-value. The importance of F-value is to show that the outcomes were not a result of sampling error or chance. Inferential statistics provide the foundation for making inferences about a population from analyses of a sample (Frankfort-Nachmias & Leon-Guerrero, 2006). Null hypotheses testing helped establish the statistical significance of the relationships between the predictor and the criterion variables and test the alternative assumptions.

An inferential statistic was calculated to assess the proportionality (linear relationship) between the predictor and criterion variables (Black, 1999). Correlation coefficients represent statistics that measure associations between two or more research variables (Flannelly, 2014). The researcher also explored multiple regression and hierarchical multiple regression analyses using IBM ® SPSS® version 24(IBM, 2016). Regression is crucial in assessing the importance of the predictors. As the most common form of data analysis Keith (2015), shared that regression analysis helps in determining whether there is a high correlation. Leedy and Ormrod (2013) defined multiple linear regressions as the ability to understand whether two or more predictors can be used to predict the criterion.

DATA ENTRY

A Microsoft® Excel® 2007 workbook spreadsheet from the Mind Garden website was downloaded and stored on a flash drive. Then the raw data were entered into five separate spreadsheets representing sections of the survey. The confirmed data were organized, coded, and transferred into spreadsheets for demographic questions, transformational and transactional subscales as well as the laissez-faire leadership, innovation, and job satisfaction scales to create variables of the study. Research data were entered into IBM® SPSS ® spreadsheets to create data files for statistical analysis.

STATISTICAL ASSUMPTIONS

Assumptions underlying the multiple regression and the Pearson correlation statistical procedures are essential for exploring the correlation between the predictor variables and the criterion variables (Zhuplatova, 2015). Researchers who are unaware of the nature of the assumptions may unintentionally produce a result that is biased or inaccurate (Newton & Rudestam, 2013). According to Hair et al. (2010), some of the assumptions that underscore a (parametric) statistical model include linearity of the measured phenomenon, normality of the error term distribution, homoscedasticity, and independence of the error terms. The assumption of linearity is important to achieve in multiple regression because the idea of correlation is based on a linear relationship best depicting a reliable prediction of the criterion variable by the predictor variables (Hair et al., 2010; Osborne & Waters, 2002).

Linearity was crucial for the analysis since Pearson's r stresses the linear relationships between variables (Newton & Rudestam, 2013). If the correlation between the predictor and the criterion variables are non-linear, the outcomes of the regression analysis will misconstrue or underrate the actual relationship (Osborne & Waters, 2002). Therefore, a researcher may add predictor variables and transform them to represent relationships to enhance or boost prediction of the criterion variable (Hair et al., 2010). The assumption of normality pertains to the multivariate normal distribution of the variables in the population to guarantee that only the linear statistical relationship exists between variables (Osborne & Waters, 2002).

Testing constant variance of the error terms is crucial to guarantee homoscedasticity of variances by employing statistical tests or residual plots (Hair et al., 2010). According to Osborne and Waters (2002), homoscedasticity "means that the variance of errors is the same across all levels of the independent variable and when the variance of errors differs," (p. 4) it indicates the presence of heteroscedasticity, which can result in severe distortion of findings and can severely debilitates the analysis. When the violation of this assumption is detected, weighted least square or transformation of the affected variables can be used (Hair et al., 2010). The independence of the error terms assumption means that the rate or worth of one observation have no impact on the rate or worth of other observations. Non-independent observations might compel statistical test to furnish too many false positives. Violation of this assumption can result in inaccurate p-values for the F-test (Hair et al., 2010). According to Zhuplatova (2015), remedies can include data transformation, integration of indicator variables or specific regression models. Evaluation of multicollinearity is critical in ensuring that no correlations among the predictor variables exist (Hair et al., 2010). Thus, a Pearson correlation was employed to measures the strength of the linear relationship between leadership style, innovation and job satisfaction.

SUMMARY

The goal of this quantitative correlational study was to understand the effect of leadership style on employee innovation and job satisfaction as indicators of success in companies that have been in business for more than 10 years, and to ascertain if there is a particular leadership style employed by leaders of XYZ retail industry organizations that have been in business for more than 10 years by encouraging and promoting innovation while other companies in the same retail industry have failed. The quantitative methodology identified the correlation between the predictor variables of leadership styles and the criterion variable of companies' success. Chapter 3 contained an assessment of the research method and design appropriateness followed with a discussion on the SIBS and MLQ Form 5X-Short (Bass & Avolio, 1995), which were used to collect data to measure innovation and job satisfaction along with leadership styles and behavior. The validity and reliability of the MLQ, SIBS instruments and the research design were examined.

The population of the XYZ organization was used to produce a convenience random sample of 84 managers and human resource personnel to participate in the study. The numerical data procured from the questionnaire was analyzed statistically. The descriptive statistics was calculated to delineate the predictor, criterion, and control variables and inferential statistics and correlational technique were employed to test the research hypotheses, achieve the purpose of the study, and answer the research questions. Participation in the study was voluntary. The chapter progressed with a conversation on participant protections, informed consent, and confidentiality in addition to sampling, data collection procedures, and rationale, instrumentation, reliability, validity, and data analysis.

A Pearson correlational analysis was applied to measure the correlation coefficient of the criterion variables to ascertain the strength and direction of the relationship. The linear relationship between the multiple predictor variables and the multiple operationalized criterion variables were analyzed using correlational and multiple regression analysis. Study results included reports and interpretation of the strength and direction of the correlations plus descriptive and inferential analysis statistics. The research design guided the analysis contained in Chapter 4, and the summary, conclusions, and recommendations presented in Chapter 5.

DATA ANALYSIS AND FINDINGS

The purpose of this quantitative correlational study was to investigate if a correlation exists between leadership style, innovation and job satisfaction as indicators of success in companies that have been in business for more than 10 years, and to ascertain if there exists a particular leadership style employed by leaders of XYZ retail industry organizations that have been in business for more than 10 years by encouraging and promoting innovation while other companies in the same retail industry have failed. The descriptive correlational research design was employed for the examination of the relationship between research variables, to answer the research questions, and attain the purpose of the study. Chapter 4 comprises an explanation of the data collection procedures, data analysis procedures, data entry, test for outliers, test for assumptions, research questions and hypotheses, the result of the study, and summary of the research findings.

RESEARCH FINDINGS

The current study results are presented by demographic data of the participants, as well as statistical analysis of data related to the hypotheses and research questions. Demographic characteristics of the participants included race, gender, education, age, tenure, and position within the organization (management or human resource personnel). Participants' gender and tenure within the organization were used as control variables in the study. A pilot study was not carried out for the study because measurement instruments validated through prior research reduce the need to test their validity (Curtis, Comiskey, & Dempsey, 2016). When instruments produce the suitable data to address the research questions, a pilot study is not needed before conducting research (Sproul, 2002).

The surveys were sent to a total of 110 participants; 84 participants completed and returned the survey with a response rate of 76.4%. After scrutinizing the data, 5 participants were rejected for not being in their current position for 5 years or longer and 2 participants were rejected for not having a high school education. In all, 77 surveys were retained for statistical analyses. The data were sufficient to support the use of multiple regression analysis in the study with three or more predictor variables, an anticipated effect size of 0.15, a desired statistical power level of 0.8, a probability level of 0.05, and a minimum required sample a size of 76 (Soper, 2015).

Table 4

Descriptive Demographic Statistics

		Age of respondents	Respondent level of education	Respondent sex	Number of years with the company
N	Valid	77	77	77	77
	Missing	0	0	0	0
Mean		1.8831	1.7532	1.5065	1.7662
Median		1.0000	2.0000		2.0000
Std. Deviation		1.06344	.71000	.50324	.74155

Note. n =77. Dummy variables: Age (1=25 -35 years, 2=36-46 years, 3=47-57 years, 4=58 and over); Gender (1=male, 2=Female); Tenure (1=5 years, 2 =6-10 years, 3=over 10 years); Education (1=high school, 2=bachelor's degree, 3=master's degree and above).

Table 4 shows that for the 77 people that participated in the surveys, the median group for respondents' age is group 1 (age =25-35 years; M=1.88, SD= 1.06); level of education is 2 (bachelor's degree; M=1.51, SD= .50) and tenure with company is group 2 (6-10 years, M=1.75, SD=.50.

Thirty-nine people between the age of 25 and 35 (51%) participated in the survey. 17 people (22%) between the age of 36 and 46 responded to the survey. Twelve (12) people between the age of 47 and 57 (16%), as well as 9 people (12%) over 58 years of age, participated in the survey. Also, 31 (40%) of people with high school education, 34 (44%) with a bachelor's degree and 12 (16%) of people with a master's degree and above responded to the survey. Additionally, 32 (42%) of the respondents had been with the company for 5years, 31 (40%) of the participants have been with the company for a period of 6 to 10 years during the survey, also, 14 (18%) of the respondents have been with the company for over 10 years.

TEST FOR OUTLIERS

Before carrying out statistical analyses, the data were tested for outliers. Outliers are observation points that are distant from other observations, and they can significantly affect statistical tests (Hair, Black, Babin & Anderson, 2010). There are several techniques for handling items that are abnormal or distant from other items, one of which is to delete the items (incomplete cases) from the sample or treat them in a manner that minimizes their potential effects on the result of the study (Borgoni & Berrington, 2013). The examination of plots representing observations of each variable and the linear relationships between predictor and criterion variables revealed the presence of outliers on the Laissez Faire scale, the Five Is of Transformational leadership scale, the satisfaction scale, and the Encourages Innovative Thinking scale. Based on the identification of outliers, observations with outlier scores for any of these scales were removed from the dataset

INFERENTIAL ANALYSES OF RESEARCH VARIABLES

A preliminary series of correlational tests were conducted to determine whether the sample of thriving organizations had leadership traits that were significantly higher or lower than the reported norm scores. A series of two multiple regression analyses were then carried out to test research hypotheses related to the relationships between predictor and criterion variables. Transformational leadership style, transactional leadership style, and laissez-faire were the predictor variables in the study. Employee innovation and employee job satisfaction were the criterion. A null hypotheses testing allowed in establishing the statistical significance of the relationships between the predictor and the criterion variables and the relative contribution of predictor variables in explaining variance in criterion variables. Multiple regression analysis furnished a means of evaluating the direction and the strengths of relationships and the significance of each predictor variable. The analysis of variance procedure was performed to test the significance of the variation in each criterion variable that may be attributed to the regression of predictor variables.

LINEAR REGRESSION ANALYSIS PREDICTING SATISFACTION

A linear regression analysis was conducted to assess whether Avoids Involvement LF, Five I's of transformational leadership, and transactional leadership significantly predicted employee satisfaction. The "Enter" variable selection method was chosen for the linear regression model, which included all of the selected predictors.

The assumptions of normality of residuals, absence of multicollinearity, the homoscedasticity of residuals, and the lack of outliers were investigated. Normality was scrutinized using a Q-Q scatterplot (figure 6) (Bates, Machler, Bolker, & Walker, 2014; DeCarlo, 1997; Field, 2014). Field (2014) recommends this plot because normality does not need to be met for the independent or dependent variable's distribution in a regression, but rather the residuals of the regression (i.e., the error between each participant's actual dependent variable value and the regression's predicted dependent variable value). The Q-Q scatterplot (figure 7) compared normal distribution of these residuals (a theoretical distribution which follows a bell curve) with the distribution of the observed residuals. In the Q-Q scatterplot, the solid line denotes the theoretical quantiles of a normal distribution. Normality can be surmised if the points form a fairly straight line. The Q-Q scatterplot for normality is presented in Figure 6. Though there was some deviation from the line indicating normality, given the sample size, it is unlikely that these deviations would cause harm to the interpretability of the results (Stevens, 2009).

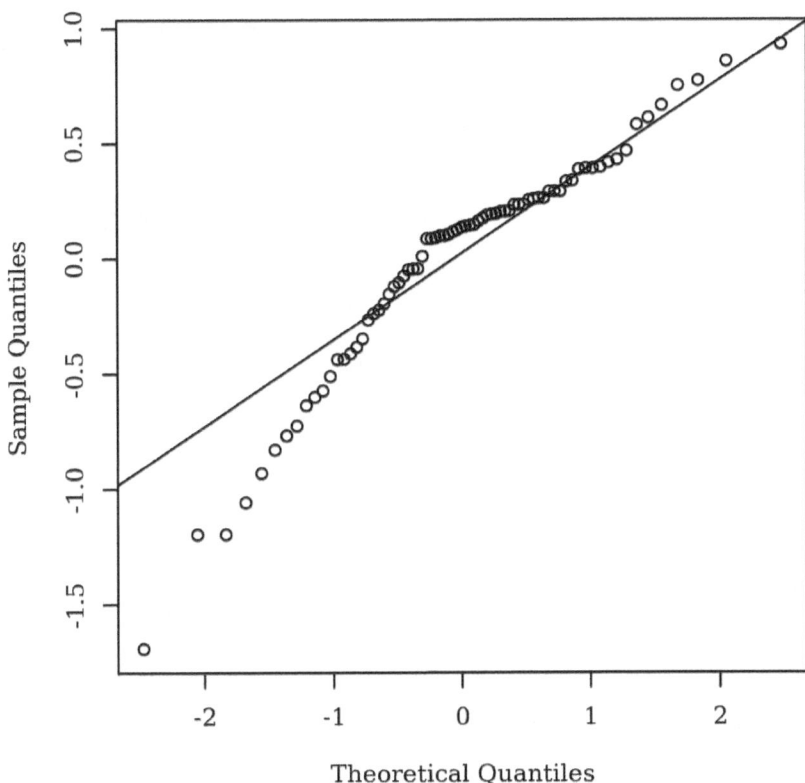

Figure 6: Q-Q scatterplot testing normality.

Homoscedasticity was assessed by plotting the predicted values against the residuals (Bates et al., 2014; Field, 2009; Osborne & Walters, 2002). The assumption of homoscedasticity would be met if the points seem randomly distributed with a mean of zero and no evidence or obvious curvature. Figure 7 presents a scatterplot of predicted values and model residuals and displays no funnel patterning that would indicate heteroscedastic data.

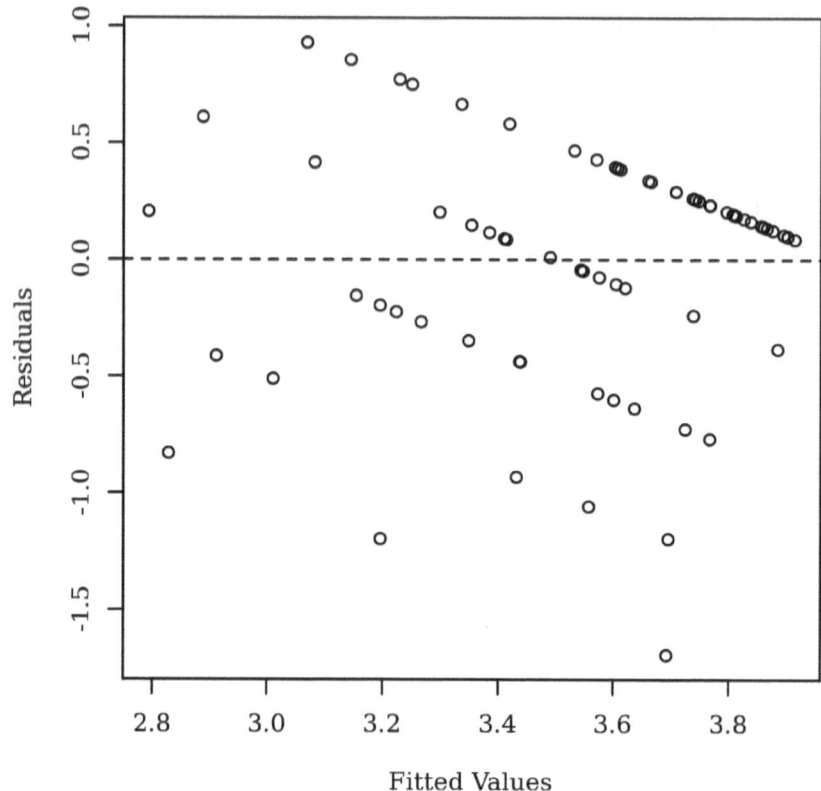

Figure 7. Residuals scatterplot testing homoscedasticity.

Finally, Variance Inflation Factors (VIFs) were calculated to uncover the presence of multicollinearity between predictors. High VIFs indicate increased effects of multicollinearity in the model. VIFs greater than 5 are cause for concern, whereas VIFs of 10 should be considered the maximum upper limit (Menard, 2009). All predictors in the regression model have VIFs less than 10, indicating that there was no cause for concern of multicollinearity. Table 5 presents the VIF for each predictor in the model.

Table 5

Variance Inflation Factors for Laissez-faire-Avoids Involvement LF,
Five I's of transformational leadership, and transactional leadership

Variable	VIF
Laissez-faire (Avoids Involvement) LF	1.53
Five I's of transformational leadership	1.56
Transactional leadership	1.29

Table 6
Regression Predicting Satisfaction F Test Output

Source	Sum of Squares	df	F	p	R^2	R^2_{adj}
Regression	5.94	3	7.63	< .001	.24	.21
Residual	18.44	71				

The results of the linear regression model were significant, $F(3, 71) = 7.63$, $p< .001$, $R^2 = 0.24$, indicating that approximately 24% of the variance in employee satisfaction SAT is explainable by the linear regression model (table 6). When we examine the individual coefficients (table 7), Laissez Laissez-faire LF was not a significant predictor of employee job satisfaction SAT, $B = 0.03$, $t(71) = 0.34$, $p = .737$. The Five I's of transformational leadership significantly predicted employee job satisfaction SAT, $B = 0.59$, $t(71) = 4.13$, $p< .001$. This indicated that on average, a one-unit increase of Five I's of transformational leadership would correspond with an increase in the value of employee job satisfaction SAT by 0.59 units. Transactional leadership did not significantly predict employee job satisfaction SAT, $B = -0.12$, $t(71) = -0.82$, $p = .414$.

Table 6 summarizes the results of the regression model.

Table 7

*Results for Linear Regression with Laissez-faire LF, Five
I's of transformational Leadership, and transactional
leadership predicting generates satisfaction SAT*

Variable	B	SE	95% CI	B	T	p
(Intercept)	1.83	0.46	[0.91, 2.74]	0.00	3.99	< .001
Laissez-faire (Avoids Involvement) LF	0.03	0.10	[-0.16, 0.23]	0.04	0.34	.737
Five I's of transformational Leadership	0.59	0.14	[0.30, 0.87]	0.53	4.13	< .001
Transactional leadership	-0.12	0.14	[-0.40, 0.17]	-.10	-.82	.414

Note. Results: F (3, 71) = 7.63, p< .001, R^2 = 0.24

*Unstandardized Regression Equation: Generates Satisfaction SAT = 1.83 +
0.03*Avoids Involvement LF + 0.59*Five I's of transformational Leadership
0.12*Transactional leadership*

LINEAR REGRESSION ANALYSIS PREDICTING ENCOURAGES INNOVATION THINKING

A second linear regression analysis was conducted to assess whether Avoids Involvement LF, Five I's of transformational leadership, and transactional leadership significantly predicted Encourages Innovative Thinking IS. The "'Enter" variable selection method was chosen for the linear regression model, which encompassed all of the selected predictors. The assumptions of normality of residuals, the absence of multicollinearity, the lack of outliers, and homoscedasticity of residuals were assessed. Normality was assessed using a Q-Q scatter plot, similar to the regression of satisfaction on leadership styles (Bates, Mächler, Bolker, & Walker, 2014; DeCarlo, 1997; Field, 2009). The Q-Q scatter plot compared a normal distribution (a theoretical distribution which follows a bell curve) with the distribution of the residuals. In the Q-Q scatter plot, the solid line signifies the theoretical quantiles of a normal distribution. Normality could be deduced if the points form a fairly straight line. The Q-Q scatter plot for normality is presented in Figure 8, and did not indicate any strong deviation from the normal line.

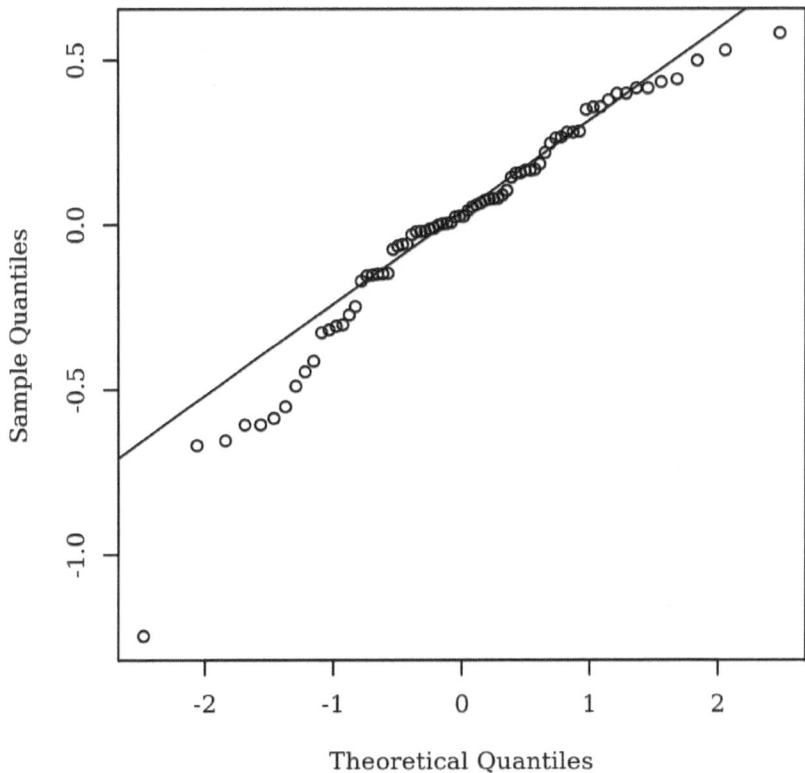

Figure 8. Q-Q scatterplot testing normality.

Homoscedasticity was assessed by plotting the predicted values against the residuals (Bates et al., 2014; Field, 2009; Osborne & Walters, 2002). The assumption of homoscedasticity would be met if the points seemed randomly distributed with a mean of zero and no evidence or obvious curvature. Figure 9 presents a scatterplot of predicted values and model residuals, and indicates that this assumption was met.

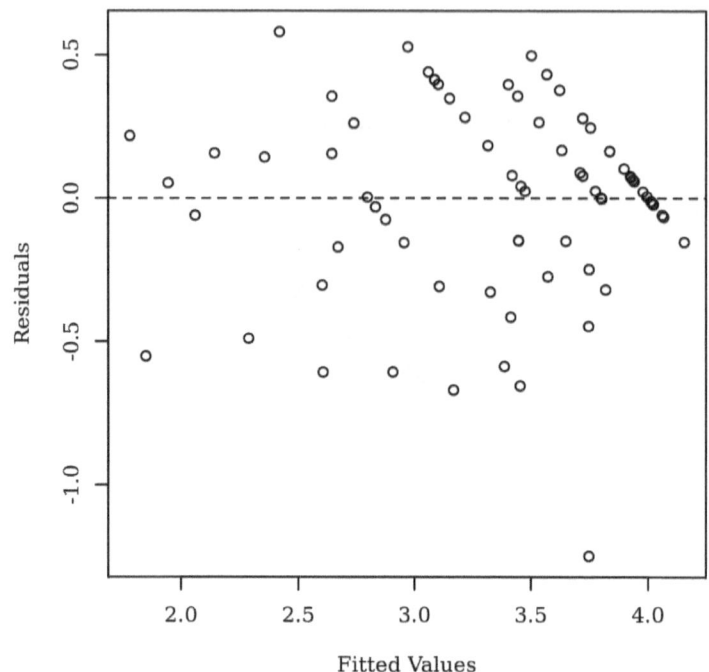

Figure 9. Residuals scatterplot testing homoscedasticity.

Variance Inflation Factors (VIFs) were calculated to detect the presence of multicollinearity between predictors. High VIFs indicate increased effects of multicollinearity in the model. VIFs greater than 5 would be cause for concern, whereas VIFs of 10 should be considered the maximum upper limit (Menard, 2009). All predictors in the regression model had VIFs less than 10. Table 13 presents the VIF for each predictor in the model.

Table 8

Variance Inflation Factors for Laissez-faire-Avoids Involvement LF,
Five I's of Transformational Leadership, and Transactional leadership

Variable	VIF
Laissez-faire (Avoids Involvement) LF	1.64
Five I's of Transformational Leadership	1.70
Transactional leadership	1.29

Table 9

Regression Predicting Encourages Innovative Thinking F Test Output

Source	Sum of Squares	df	F	p	R^2	R^2_{adj}
Regression	26.72	3	77.62	< .001	.76	.75
Residual	8.26	72				

The results of the linear regression model were significant, F (3, 72) = 77.62, $p < .001$, $R^2 = 0.76$, indicating that approximately 76% of the variance in *Encourages Innovative Thinking*-IS explained by the model. Laissez-faire (Avoids involvement LF) did not significantly predict *Encourages Innovative Thinking*-IS, $B = 0.03$, t (72) = 0.51, $p = .609$. Five I's of transformational leadership significantly predicted *Encourages Innovative Thinking*-IS, $B = 1.15$, t (72) = 12.21, $p < .001$. This indicated that on average, a one-unit increase of Five I's of transformational leadership would increase the value of *Encourages Innovative Thinking*-IS (intellectual stimulation) by 1.15 units. Transactional leadership did not significantly predict *Encourages Innovative Thinking*, $B = -0.11$, t (72) = -1.13, $p = .263$. Table 9 summarizes the results of the linear regression model.

Table 10

Results for Linear Regression with Laissez-faire-LF, Five I's of transformational leadership, and transactional leadership predicting Encourages Innovative Thinking-IS

Variable	B	SE	95% CI	β	T	p
(Intercept)	0.19	0.30	[-0.79, .41]	0.00	-.64	.523
Laissez-faire (Avoids-Involvement) LF	0.03	0.06	[-0.10, 0.16]	0.04	0.51	.609
Five I's of Transformational Leadership	1.15	0.09	[0.96, 1.33]	0.91	12.2	<.001
Transactional leadership	-.11	0.10	[-0.30, 0.08]	-.07	-.13	.263

Note. Results: F (3, 72) = 77.62, p< .001, R² = 0.76

Unstandardized Regression Equation: Encourages Innovative Thinking-IS= -0.19 + 0.03*Avoids Involvement-LF + 1.15*Five I's of transformational leadership 0.11*Transactional leadership

FINDINGS RELATED TO THE RESEARCH QUESTIONS.

RQ1. What is the relationship between leadership style and job satisfaction in companies that have been in business for more than 10 years? Two hypotheses associated with this research question were tested.

H1$_a$: Leadership style will be positively associated with job satisfaction in companies that have been in business for more than 10 years.

H1$_0$: Leadership style will not be positively associated with job satisfaction in companies that have been in business for more than 10 years.

Transformational leadership was the only significant component of the regression predicting satisfaction $F (3, 71) =7.627$, $p <.001$, $R^2= .244$, adj. $R^2 = .212$. Given a correlation significant at the 0.01 level, it means that there is a positive correlation between the transformational leadership and companies that have been in business for more than 10 years when using satisfaction as an indicator of organizational success. Thus, it is statistically significant, and the null hypothesis is rejected. According to Greenland et al. (2016), in a hypothesis or probability testing, if the p-value is ≤ .05 (alpha level), the null hypothesis is rejected, and the alternative hypothesis is tentatively accepted for transformational leadership style. H1$_0$was not rejected for Transactional and laissez-faire leadership styles.

RQ2. What is the relationship between leadership style and innovation in companies that have been in business for more than 10 years?

H2$_a$: Leadership style will be positively associated with innovation in companies that have been in business for more than 10 years.

H2$_0$: Leadership style will not be positively associated with innovation in companies that have been in business for more than 10 years.

The outcomes of the hypotheses-testing demonstrated a significantly positive relationship between transformational leadership style and employee innovation in samples of the companies that have been in business for more than 10 years, $F (3, 72) = 77.620$, $p< .001$, $R^2 = 0.764$, adjusted $R^2 = 0.754$. Thus, H2$_0$ was rejected for a transformational leadership style. Given the two p-values for transactional and laissez faire leadership (i.e., $p = .263$ and $p = .609$ respectively), findings indicated that transactional leadership and laissez-faire leadership among companies that have been in business for more than 10 years were not significantly predictive of employee innovation. Therefore, H2$_0$ relating to transactional and laissez-faire leadership styles was not rejected for these variables.

SUMMARY

The aim of chapter 4 was to present the research findings relating to the study's research questions and hypotheses. Chapter 4 commenced with a detailed explanation of the data collection procedures, the data analysis procedures, a description of data entry, and the research findings sections includes a description of outcomes of descriptive analyses of demographic data, test for outliers, and test for the assumptions underlying statistical analysis. Chapter 4 also contains sections relevant to the research questions and the results of the hypotheses testing. Multiple regression analysis furnished a means of evaluating the direction and the strengths of correlations and the relative significance of each predictor variable, while correlation tests allowed the researcher to determine the traits of leadership within the sample of companies that have been in business for more than 10 years. In essence, there was strong evidence that the samples of the companies that have been in business for more than 10 years have a significantly higher degree of transformational leadership, and that these levels of leadership are positively related to both satisfaction in the company and innovation within the company. Only transformational leadership was positively associated with innovation and job satisfaction in companies that have been in business for more than 10 years. The results of the study are further discussed in chapter 5, which also encompasses a summary of research findings, an explanation of strengths and limitations of the study, implications for leadership, recommendations for future research, and conclusion.

CONCLUSION

Chapter 4 encompassed a description/account of research findings of the quantitative descriptive correlational study. The purpose of the study was to understand the effect of leadership style on innovation and job satisfaction as indicators of success in companies that have been in business for more than 10 years, and to ascertain if there exists a particular leadership style employed by leaders of XYZ retail industry organizations that have been in business for more than 10 years by encouraging and promoting innovation while other companies in the same retail industry have failed. A detailed examination or investigation of statistical relationships between variables was carried out to answer the study research questions and attain the purpose of the study. Preparatory analyses were carried out before testing the research hypotheses. A multiple regression analysis was used as a method/technique for examining relationships between predictor and criterion variables and the relative benefaction of each predictor variable.

The results of hull hypotheses-testing indicated significant positive relationships between transformational leadership style, employee job satisfaction, and employee innovation in XYZ companies that have been in business for more than 10 years. The analyses did not identify significant relationships between transactional leadership and laissez-faire leadership with employee job satisfaction and employee innovation in XYZ companies.

CHAPTER 5

CONCLUSIONS AND RECOMMENDATIONS

The quantitative, descriptive correlational research study geared toward understanding if there exist a correlation between leadership style, innovation and job satisfaction as indicators of success in companies that have been in business for more than 10 years, and to ascertain if there exists a particular leadership style employed by leaders of XYZ retail industry organizations that have been in business for more than 10 years by encouraging and promoting innovation while other companies in the same retail industry have failed. A theoretical framework furnished the foundation for the research questions and reasons/justifications for the application of correlational research design and regression analysis for investigating the conceptualized correlations between research variables. The theoretical integration of the transactional and transformational leadership theory (Bass 1999), the concept of employee satisfaction (Allen, & Meyer, 1990), social exchange theory (Blau, 1964), and attitude theories (Fishbein & Ajzen, 1975; Rosenberg & Hovland, 1960) were used to interpret research findings. Chapter 5encompasses a summary of research findings, an explanation of the strengths and limitations of the study, implications for leadership, recommendations for future research, and conclusion.

SUMMARY OF RESEARCH FINDINGS

The general problem was retail industry organizations that have not been in business for more than 10 years continues to struggle, despite a plethora of information regarding the importance of leadership styles (transformational, transactional, and laissez-faire), and the effects on innovation and job satisfaction (Ojukuku et al., 2012). The specific problem was retail industry organizational leaders do not understand the effect of leadership style on innovation and job satisfaction as indicators of success in companies that have been in business for more than 10 years (Bowonder, Dambal, Kumar, & Shirodkar, 2010). Many studies on different leadership styles have been conducted (Bhatti, Nawab, & Akbar, 2011; Schin, & Racovita, 2013), only a few have been able to demonstrate the effectiveness of leadership practice (transformational, transactional, laissez-faire) and none have been able to pinpoint the dominant style used by leaders to successfully promote and improve employee innovation and job satisfaction within the retail industry (Schin & Racovita, 2013).

The purpose of this quantitative correlational study was to investigate if a correlation exists between leadership style, innovation and job satisfaction as indicators of success in companies that have been in business for more than 10 years. And to ascertain if there was a dominant leadership style used by leaders of XYZ retail industry organizations that have been in business for more than 10 years. The study method was considered appropriate for ascertaining whether correlations existed between the variables used to test the hypotheses (Leedy & Ormrod, 2010; Neuman, 2011).

Transformational leadership style, transactional leadership style, and laissez-faire leadership style formed the predictor variables, while innovation and job satisfaction were the factors used to describe the criterion variable that determines organizational success. The Statistics Canada's Survey of Innovation and Business Strategy (SIBS) and three MLQ survey instruments were used to gather and analyze data - the MLQ Leader Form, the MLQ Rater Form, and the MLQ Scoring Key Form 5x to capture and measure full-range leadership theory styles. Measured with the MLQ 5x-Short, employee rater perceptions of their leaders and owner/leader self-perceptions were inspected for the operationalized criterion variables of (a) effectiveness, (b) satisfaction with leadership, and (c) extra effort (motivation). Participants were also asked to complete a demographic survey in addition to SIBS and MLQ surveys.

FINDINGS RELATED TO THE RESEARCH QUESTIONS

The research questions presented throughout the chapters set the path and direction for addressing the research problem to evaluate the relationship of leadership to the operationalized criterion variables. Two research questions are presented in relation to the literature review and pertinent theories. Also, two null hypotheses and two alternative hypotheses aided in testing the research questions.

Findings related to RQ1: What is the relationship between leadership style and job satisfaction in companies that have been in business for more than 10 years? The results of the hypotheses-testing provided the following answer to the research question 1. Transformational leadership style was significantly positive to employee job satisfaction in XYZ companies that have been in business for more than 10 years. This finding supports the transformational theory that allows followers to ascend to the highest extent of fulfillment than believed practicable and elevate followers' dedication toward supporting the leader's dream, assuming more responsibility, creating innovative techniques, and performing more efficiently (Bowonder et al., 2010). It also supports and assists followers to develop and sprout into leaders by paying attention to their needs, empowering, and aligning the goals and objectives of each person, the group, the leader, and the larger organization (Hickman, 2016, p. 76).

The same hypotheses testing also indicated that among companies that have been in business for more than 10 years, transactional leadership style as well as laissez-faire leadership among companies that have been in business for more than 10 years were not significantly positive to job satisfaction. The finding agrees with the transactional theory which requires an interchange procedure that brings about follower adherence to leader desire but is unlikely to produce commitment and enthusiasm to the mission objective (Hickman, 2016). Similarly, the finding supports laissez-faire leadership theory which says that leaders pay no attention to the needs of subordinates, does not manage employee performance, and does not respond to problems (Bass, 1985; Yukl, 2013). Laissez-faire does not represent leadership because of leaders' avoidance of involvement in conflict resolution, interaction with subordinates, and lack of interest at events around them. Laissez-faire leaders are unapproachable and believe that employees are capable of solving problems on their own (Hickman, 2016).

Findings related to RQ2: What is the relationship between leadership style and innovation in companies that have been in business for more than 10 years? The results of the hypotheses-testing demonstrated a significant positive relationship between transformational leadership style and employee innovation in samples of the companies that have been in business for more than 10 years. The results confirmed that the transformational leadership style promotes employee innovation (Bowonder et al., 2010). The findings also indicated that transactional leadership and laissez-faire leadership among companies that have been in business for more than 10 years were not significantly positive to employee innovation. In conclusion, answers to the two research questions revealed that though each leadership style plays a crucial role in organizational success, transformational leadership is a dominant leadership style used by leaders of XYZ retail industry organizations that have been in business for more than 10 years. The present finding is parallel or congruent with the belief that employees favor facets of transformational leadership style that encourage a sense of moral obligation over laissez-faire and transactional leadership style which purely relies on utilizing contingent reward and feedback (Bass, 1985). It promotes employees and development and provides opportunities for professional and personal growth (Bass, 1999).

Strengths and Limitations of the Study. The research study was devised to survey a sample of members of two small retail companies to examine and understand the effect of leadership style on employee innovation and job satisfaction and to ascertain if there was a dominant leadership style used by leaders of XYZ retail industry organizations that have been in business for more than 10 years. The correlational research design and quantitative research methodology taking into account the endorsed statistical procedures established validity and reliability for greater objectivity and accuracy of research findings (Harwell, 2011).

The implementation of standards used in quantitative research as well as the use of random probability sampling method where members of the population had an equal probability of being chosen (Boni, Silva, Bastos,

Pechansky, & Vasconcellos, 2012) increased the likelihood of the sample representing the population as a whole. Stratified sampling was also explored because of the heterogeneity and demography of the population. The effect size, the power of the statistical test, and the number of parameters used in testing the research hypotheses warrant/allow replications of the study and juxtapositions of the results with similar studies (Babbie, 2010). In addition to these strengths, the study also had a limitation which was associated with the survey participants. Survey participants who included the managers and human resource personnel that originally agreed to participate before the surveys were emailed decided not to participate anymore because there was no financial benefit for their services and that reduced the sample size of the study.

Implications for Leadership. Current and germinal sources of the literature confirmed positive relationships between transformational leadership, job satisfaction and innovation in various organizations (Tohidi & Jabbari, 2012; Holdnak et al., 1993). Employee job satisfaction is an essential job enrichment related to countless positive outcomes in an organization. The role leadership style play in the development of employee dedication and allegiance to an organization cannot be overemphasized. The results of some germinal and current research studies revealed that transformational leadership style of managers or directors had been a significant factor that decisively affects the nature and the degree of employee organizational allegiance, performance, productivity, retention, or commitment (Schin & Racovita, 2013). This study expanded knowledge about the relationship between leadership style, employee innovation and job satisfaction as measures of organizational success.

Findings of prior studies indicated that transformational leaders contribute to building dedicated and continuance allegiance of their subordinates in organizations (Schin & Racovita, 2013). The current study's findings disclosed evidence of significant relationships between transformational leadership style of XYZ company directors and employee innovation and job satisfaction as the reasons behind their competitiveness and continued success. Understanding the dominant leadership style adopted by some of these successful leaders in their various organizations could be an invaluable asset to millions of leaders worldwide.

RECOMMENDATIONS

The current study furnished insight into the problem of failures of some retail industry organization through the application of effective or ineffective leadership style of directors to enhance employee organizational allegiance and develop a competitive advantage through employee innovation and job satisfaction. Research findings inform the research problem leading to the study and assist the development of knowledge in the field of organizational and industrial psychology. Recommendations for future research and conclusion are based on the study results.

Recommendation for future Research. The focal point of the present descriptive correlational study was on the examination of multivariate relationships between leadership styles of transformational, transactional, laissez-faire, and employee innovation and job satisfaction as measures of organizational success; to ascertain if there is a dominant leadership style used by leaders of retail industry organization that have been in business for more than 10 years. The examination of the relationships involved the assessment of the transformational leadership style, transactional leadership style and laissez-faire leadership style in enhancing or encouraging employee innovation and job satisfaction that brings about competitive advantage and organizational success. Significant positive relationships were found between transformational leadership style and employee innovation and between transformational leadership style and job satisfaction.

The results are concurrent with previous research findings that transformational leadership promotes employee innovation and job satisfaction (Tohidi & Jabbari, 2012; Holdnak et al., 1993). There are not enough studies involving a transformational leadership style and its impact on innovation and job satisfaction. Future studies can examine these relationships in big business organizations to validate the current findings using a qualitative research method. Concerning laissez-faire leadership, there were not enough sources of the literature examining neither relationship between laissez-faire leadership style and organizational success nor its impact on innovation and job satisfaction. A more inclusive model with a broader perspective on leadership behavior (Michel et al., 2011) and a complete model of the factors that explains the leader organizational performance link are recommended. Recommendations for future research also include studies of a broader range geographic locations and business sectors to access a more diverse population and mixed or qualitative research methods to identify factors that were not included in the current study should be exploded to shed more insight.

Also, future research can further investigate the relationships between transactional leadership strategies and employee innovation. Research findings regarding the benefaction of the transactional leadership style in describing the discrepancy or variation in the level of employee innovation and satisfaction above the transformational leadership style were not explored or expatiated. Therefore, investigating the relationship between the transactional leadership strategies contingent reward and management-by-exception active and innovation may furnish significant results. Future research studies with larger sample size and robust research design can supply findings that are generalizable to other settings and populations. The assertion that successful leaders incorporate both transformational and transactional style (Bass, 1985) can also be tested in future research. Similar studies in different organizations can furnish additional findings and add to the body of knowledge related to the effect of leadership style on innovation and job satisfaction as indicators of organizational success.

This quantitative, descriptive correlational research study was geared toward understanding the effect of leadership style on innovation and job satisfaction as indicators of success in companies that have been in business for more than 10 years, and to ascertain if there exists a particular leadership style employed by leaders of XYZ retail industry organizations that have been in business for more than 10 years by encouraging and promoting innovation while other companies in the same retail industry have failed. To ascertain the relationship between the variables, statistical tests were performed on data collected from the Statistics of Canada's Survey of Innovation and Business Strategy (SIBS) submitted through Survey Monkey and from Multifactor Leadership Questionnaire (MLQ) survey submitted through a Mind Garden Transform website by 77 participants.

The results indicated a significant positive relationship between transformational leadership style and employee innovation and a significant positive correlation between transformational leadership style and employee job satisfaction, the two measure of organizational success in the study. Conversely, a significant negative relationship was detected between transactional leadership style and employee innovation as well as a significant negative relationship between transactional leadership and employee job satisfaction. The results also indicated a negative relationship between laissez-faire leadership style and employee innovation as well as a negative relationship between laissez-faire leadership style and employee job satisfaction. Because transformational leadership style showed positive significance with employee innovation and job satisfaction in XYZ companies that have been in business for more than 10 years which indicated organizational success. It was concluded that the transformational leadership style is the dominant leadership style used by leaders of the XYZ retail industry organization that have been in business for more than 10 years. However, a more inclusive model with a broader perspective on leadership behavior (Michel, Lyons & Cho, 2011) and a comprehensive model of the factors that explain the leader organizational performance link are recommended. Recommendations for further research include studies of a broader range of business sectors and geographic locations to access a more diverse population and mixed or qualitative research methods to identify factors that were not included in the current study should be explored to shed more insight.

SUMMARY

This quantitative correlational study was an investigation of the correlation between leadership styles, innovation and job satisfaction as expounded by full-range leadership theory known as transformational, transactional, and laissez-faire, of XYZ retail industry organization that have been in business for more than 10 years in the metropolitan Detroit area. The Pearson correlation and linear regression analysis was performed to examine the correlation between leadership styles (transformational, transactional and laissez-faire), innovation and job satisfaction as indicators of organizational success. The study also ascertained the dominant leadership style used by the leaders of the XYZ retail industry organization that have been in business for more than 10 years.

The results of the Pearson correlation and linear regression analyses provided measures of correlations between each predictor and each criterion variable indicating the level and the direction of the correlation between these variables. The results indicated a significant positive relationship between transformational leadership style and employee innovation and a significant positive correlation between transformational leadership style and employee job satisfaction, the two measure of organizational success in the study. Conversely, a significant negative relationship was detected between transactional leadership style and employee innovation as well as a significant negative relationship between transactional leadership and employee job satisfaction. The results also indicated a negative relationship between laissez-faire leadership style and employee innovation as well as a negative relationship between laissez-faire leadership style and employee job satisfaction. Because transformational leadership style showed positive significance with employee innovation and job satisfaction in XYZ companies that have been in business for more than 10 years which indicated organizational success. It was concluded that the transformational leadership style is the dominant leadership style used by leaders of the XYZ retail industry organization that have been in business for more than 10 years.

CONCLUSION

Chapter 5 contained a description/summary of research findings of the quantitative correlational study. The purpose of the study was to understand the effect of leadership style on innovation and job satisfaction as indicators of success in companies that have been in business for more than 10 years, and to ascertain if there exists a particular leadership style employed by leaders of XYZ retail industry organizations that have been in business for more than 10 years while other companies in the same retail industry have failed. The review of relevant scholarship and theoretical framework provided the foundation for the research questions and the justification for the use of the correlational research design and regression analysis for investigating theoretical relationships between research variables. Inferential, descriptive statistics and correlational were employed to assess the relationship between the variables, test hypotheses and draw conclusions about the population based on the sample and to describe data sets with summary figures and tables (Greenland et al., 2014). According to Hair et al. (2010), correlation is appropriate if the goal of the research is to establish the relationship between two or more dependent variables. The examination of statistical relationships provided the research findings that were used to answer the research questions and achieve the purpose of the study.

Significant positive relationships were found between transformational leadership style and employee innovation and transformational leadership style of directors and managers and employee job satisfaction in two small retail industry organizations. A significant positive relationship was not found between the transactional style of directors and managers of the two XYZ retail industry organizations and employee innovation and job satisfaction. Similarly, a significant positive relationship was not found between laissez-faire leadership style of directors and managers of the two XYZ retail industry organizations. The transformational, transactional and laissez-faire leadership theory (Bass 1999), concept of organizational commitment (Allen, & Meyer, 1990), attitude theories (Fishbein & Ajzen, 1975; Rosenberg & Hovland, 1960), and social exchange theory (Blau, 1964) were employed in the interpretation of the research findings.

The results of the study underpinned the proclamation that the nature of the relationship between transactional and transformational leadership style and outcomes are not the same in different organizational contexts (Howell & Avolio, 1993; Bass, 1990). The findings may expound the underlying logic of organizational activities to help organization members evaluate workplace strategies that lead to organizational success. The results may also enhance the creation and advancement of innovations that organizations need to maintain and remain competitive.

REFERENCES

Allen, N. J., & Meyer, J. P. (1990). The measurement and antecedents of affective, continuance and normative commitment to the organization. *Journal of Occupational Psychology, 63*(1), 1-18. doi: 10.1111/j.2044-8325.1990. tb00506.x

Altman, D. G., & Bland, J. M. (2009). Parametric vs. non-parametric methods for data. *British Medical Journal, 338,* doi: 10.1136/bmj. a3167

Amah, E. & Ahiauzu, A. (2013). Employee involvement and organizational effectiveness. *Journal of Management Development,* 32(7); 661-674. doi.org/10.1108/ JMD-09-2010-0064

Amissah, E. F., Gamor, E., Deri, M. N., & Amissah, A. (2016). Factors influencing employee job satisfaction in Ghana's hotel industry. *Journal of Human Resources in Hospitality & Tourism,* 15(2); 166-183. doi:10.1080/15332845.2016.1084858

Andries, P., & Czarnitzki, D. (2014). Small firm innovation performance and employee involvement. *Small Business Economic,* 43(1); 21-38. doi 10.1007/s11187-014-9577-1

Avolio, B. J., & Bass, B. M. (2004). *Multifactor leadership questionnaire. Manual and sampler test* (3a ed.). Redwood City, CA: Mind Garden

Aziz, H. H. A., & Rizkallah, A. (2015). Effect of organizational factors on employees' generation of innovative ideas: Empirical study on the Egyptian software development industry. *EuroMed Journal of Business,* 10(2); 134-146, doi: 10.1108/EMJB-12-2014-0044

Baah, K. D. & Mekpor, B. (2017). The leaders' emotional intelligence: An antecedent of employees' voluntary workplace behavior. Evidence from the Ghanaian banking sector. *African Journal of Economic and Management Studies, 8(3); 352,* https://doi.org/10.1108/AJEMS-05-2016-0066

Babbie, E. R. (2010). *The practice of social research* (12th ed.). Belmont, CA: Wadsworth Publishing Company

Barling, J., Weber, T., & Kelloway, E. K. (1996). Effects of transformational leadership training on attitudinal and financial outcomes: A field experiment. *Journal of Applied Psychology, 81*(6), 827-832. doi: 10.1037/0021-9010.81.6.827

Bass, B. M. (1985). *Leadership and performance beyond expectations.* New York, NY: Free Press.

Bass, B. M. (1999). Two decades of research and development in transformational leadership. *European Journal of Work and Organizational Psychology, 8*(1), 9–32. Retrieved from http://www.techtied.net/wpcontent/uploads/2007/10/bass_transforrmational_leadership.pdf

Bass, B. M., & Avolio, B. J. (1994). *Improving organizational effectiveness through transformational leadership.* Thousand Oaks, CA: Sage Publications

Bass, B. M. (1990). From transactional to transformational leadership: Learning to share the vision. Organizational Dynamics, 18(3), 19-31. https://doi.org/10.1016/0090-2616(90)90061-S

Bass, B. M., & Avolio, B. J. (1995). Multifactor leadership questionnaire. Retrieved from http://www.mindgarden.com/16-multifactor-leadership-questionnaireI

Bass, B.M. and Avolio, B. J. (2000). *MLQ Multifactor Leadership Questionnaire Technical Report,* Sage, Thousand Oaks, CA. [Google Scholar]

Bates, D., Mächler, M., Bolker, B., & Walker, S. (2014). Fitting linear mixed-effects models using lme4. *arXiv preprint arXiv:1406.5823.*

Belzung, C. (2014). Empathy. *Journal of Perspectives of Economic Political and Social Integration,* 19(1); 177-191. doi.org/10.2478/v10241-012-0016-4

Bhatti, K. K., Nawab, S., & Akbar, A. (2011). Effect of direct participation on organizational commitment. *International Journal of Business and Social Science, 2*(9), 15-23. Retrieved from www.ijbssnet.com

Bigliardi, B., & Galati, F. (2014). The implementation of TQM in R & D environments: *Journal of Technology Management & Innovation, 9*(2), 157-171. doi:10.4067/S0718-27242014000200012

Black, T. R. (1999). *Doing quantitative research in the social sciences: An integrated approach to research, design, measurement, and statistics.* Thousand Oaks, CA: Sage Publications.

Blanchard, K. H., & Johnson, D. E. (2008). *Management of organizational behavior (*9th ed.*)* Upper Saddle River, NJ: Education, Inc

Blau, P. M. (1964). Exchange and power in social life. New York, NY: Wiley

Bon, A. T., & Mustafa, E. M. A. (2013). Impact of total quality management on innovation in service organizations: Literature review and new conceptual framework. *Procedia Engineering, 53,* 516-529. doi:10.1016/j. proeng. 2013.02.067

Bono, J. E., & Judge, T. A. (2004). Personality and transformational and transactional leadership: A meta-analysis. Journal of Applied Psychology, 89(5), 901-910. doi: 10.1037/0021-9010.89.5.901

Boni, R. D., Silva, L. D., Bastos, F. I., Pechansky, F., Vasconcellos, T. L. (2012). Reaching the hard-to-reach: A probability sampling method for assessing prevalence of driving under the influence after drinking in alcohol outlets: *Plos One; San Francisco, 7*(4); e34104. doi: 10.1371/journal.pone.0034104

Borgoni, R. & Berrington, A. (2013). Evaluating a sequential tree-based procedure for multivariate imputation of complex missing data structures. *Journal of Qual Quant, 47(); 1991-2008.* DOI 10.1007/s11135-011-9638-3

Bowonder, B., Dambal, A., Kumar, S., & Shirodkar, A. (2010). Innovation strategies for creating competitive advantage. *Research Technology Management, 53*(3); 19-32. https://doi.org/10.1080/08956308.2010.11657628

Brown, D. R. (2011). *An experiential approach to organization development* (8ᵗʰ ed.). Upper Saddle River, NJ: Prentice Hall.

Buckingham, M. (2005). *The one thing you need to know about great managing, great leading, and sustained individual success.* New York, NY: Simon & Schuster.

Buckley, P. F. & Curd, N. D. (2012). Administrative skills in psychiatry: Leadership and career development. *Journal of Psychiatric Administration and Management,* 1(2); 69-72. Retrieved fromproquest.com

Chadwick, S. A. (2016). Can University leaders manage the tensions between the practice of innovation and the traditions of the University? *Journal of Leadership Studies, 10*(1), 80-81.doi:10.1002/jls.21456

Charbonneau, D., Barling, J., & Kelloway, E. K. (2001). Transformational leadership and sports performance: The mediating role of intrinsic motivation. *Journal of Applied Social Psychology,* 31(7); 1521-1534. doi: 10.1111/j.1559-1816. 2001.tb02686.x

Cho, Y. J., & Perry, J. L. (2012). Intrinsic motivation and employee attitudes role of managerial trustworthiness, goal directedness, and extrinsic reward expectancy. *Review of Public Personnel Administration,* 32(4); 382-406. doi: 10.1177/0734371X11421495

Collins, S. J. (2001). *Good to great: Why some companies make the leap...and others don't.* New York, NY: HarperCollins Publishers

Collins, C. G., Gibson, C. B., Quigley, N. R., & Parker, S. K. (2016). Unpacking team dynamics with growth modeling: An approach to test, refine, and integrate theory. *Organizational Psychology Review SAGE production,* 6(1); 63-91.doi: 10.1177/2041386614561249

Cornelison, P. (2013). The effectiveness of total quality management principles in the printing industry. Retrieved from http://digitalcommons.calpoly.edu/grcsp/92

Curtis, E. A., Comiskey, C. & Dempsey, O. (2016). Importance and use of correlationalresearch. *Royal College of Nursing Publishing Company (RCN), 23*(6), 20-25. doi:10.7748/nr. 2016.e1382

DeCarlo, L. T. (1997). On the meaning and use of kurtosis. *Psychological methods*, 2(3), 292-307

Delanty, G., & Strydom, P. (2003). *Philosophies of social science: The class and contemporary readings.* Philadelphia, PA: McGraw-Hill House

Denison, D. R., Hooijberg, R., & Quinn, R. E. (1995). Paradox and performance: Toward a theory of behavioral complexity in managerial leadership. *Journal of Organization Science*, 6, 524-540. doi:10.1287/orsc.6.5.524

De Winter, J. C. F. & Dodou, D. (2010). Five-Point Likert Items: t test versus Mann-Whitney-Wilcoxon. *Practical Assessment, Research & Evaluation*. 15(11), 1-16

Dyer, W. G., Dyer, J. H., & Dyer, W. G. (2013). *Team building: Proven strategies for improving team performance* (5th ed.). San Francisco, CA: Wiley

Eisenbeiss, S. A., Van Knippenberg, D., Boerner, S. (2008). Transformational leadership and team innovation: Integrating team climate principles. *Journal of Applied Psychology*, 93(6), 1438-1446. doi:10.1037/a0012716

Ekelund, H. (2015, August 1). Why some CEOs fail, and others succeed [Weblog post]. Retrieved from https://www.bts.com/news-insights/strategy-execution-blog/news-and-press-releases/why-some-ceos-fail-and-others-succeed

Emery, C. R., & Barker, K. J. (2007). The effect of transactional and transformational leadership styles on the organizational commitment and job satisfaction of customer contact personnel. *Journal of Organizational Culture, Communication and Conflict*, 11(1), 77-83. Retrieved from http://www.alliedacademies.org/Publications/Papers/JOCCC%20Vol%2011%20 No%201%202007%20p%2077-90.pdf

Farrugia, P., Petrisor, B., Farrokhyar, F., & Bhandari, M. (2010). Practical tips for surgical research: Research questions, hypotheses and objectives. *Canadian Journal of Surgery*, 53, 278-281 Retrieved from https://www.researchgate.net/publication

Field, A. (2014). *Discovering statistics using IBM SPSS statistics* (4th ed.). Thousand Oaks, CA: Sage Publications

Field, A. (2009). *Discovering statistics using SPSS*. Thousand Oaks, CA: Sage publications.

Fiedler, F. E., & Garcia, J. E. (1987). *New approach to effective leadership*. New York, NY: John Wiley.

Fishbein, M., & Ajzen, I. (1975). *Belief, attitude, intention, and behavior: An introduction to theory and research*. Reading, MA: Addison-Wesley.

Flannelly, L. T. (2014). Independent, dependent, and other variables in healthcare and chaplaincy research. *Journal of Health Care Chaplaincy, 20* (4), 161-170. doi: 10.1080/08854726.2014.959374

Fleenor, J. W. (2011). Trait approach to leadership. In S. G. Rogelberg (Ed.), *Encyclopedia of Industrial and Organizational Psychology*. Thousand Oaks, CA: Sage Publications.

Fleishman, E. A. (1953). The description of supervisory behavior. *Journal of Applied Psychology, 37,* 181-210. doi:10.1037/h0056314

Frank, B., Eckrich, H., & Rohr, J. (1997). Quality nursing care: Leadership makes the difference. *Journal of Nursing Administration, 27*(5), 13-14. doi: 10.1097/00005110-199705000-00004

Frankfort-Nachmias, C, & Leon-Guerrero, A. (2006). *Social statistics for a diverse society* (4th ed.). Thousand Oaks, CA: Sage Publication, Inc.

Frooman, J., Mendelson, M. B., & Murphy, J. K. (2012). Transformational and passive avoidant leadership as determinants of absenteeism. *Leadership and Organization Development Journal, 33*(5), 447-463. doi: 10.1108/01437731211241247

Gharakhani, D., Rahmati, H., Farrokhi, M. R., & Farahmandian, A. (2013). Total quality management and organizational performance. *American Journal of Industrial Engineering*1(3), 46-50. doi:10.1269/ ajie-1-3-2

Gill, E. (2016, October 19). *What is laissez-faire leadership? How autonomy can drive success*. Retrieved from http://online.stu.edu/ laissez-faire-leadership/

Gillespie, N. A., & Mann, L. (2004). Transformational leadership and shared values: The building blocks of trust. *Journal of Managerial Psychology*, 19, 588-601. doi:10.1108/02683940410551507

Goleman, D. (1998). What makes a leader? *Harvard Business Review, 76*, 93–102. Retrieved from www.hbr.org

Gooty, J., Connelly, S., Griffith, J., & Gupta, A. (2010). Leadership affect and emotions: A state of the science review. *The Leadership Quarterly*, 21(6); 979-1004. doi: 10.1016/j.leaqua.2010.10.005

Greenland, S., Senn, S. J., Rothman, K. J., Carlin, J. B., Poole, C., Goodman, S. N., & Altman, D. G. (2016). Statistical tests, P values, confidence intervals, and power: a guide to misinterpretations. *European Journal of Epidemiology, 31*(4). 337-350. doi: 10.1007/s10654-016-0149-3

Greenwald, H. P. (2008). *Organizations: Management without control.* Thousand Oaks: Sage Publications.

Gurdjian, P., Halbeisen, T., & Lane, K. (2014). Why leadership-development programs fail. *McKinsey Quarterly*, (1), 121-126. Retrieved from EBSCOhost Publications

Gupta, S. K. (2012). The relevance of confidence interval and *P*-value in inferential statistics. *Indian Journal of Pharmacology, 44*, 143-144. doi:10.4103/0253-7613.91895

Harwell, M. R. (2011). Chapter 10: Research design in quantitative, qualitative, mixed methods. In C. F. Conrad & R. C. Serlin (Eds.). *The Sage handbook for research and education: Pursuing ideas as the keystone of exemplary inquiry* (2nd ed.). Retrieved from http://www.sagepub.com/upm-data/41165_10.pdf

Hair, J. F., Black, W. C., Babin, B. J., & Anderson, R. E. (2010). *Multivariate data analysis* (7th ed.). Upper Saddle River, NJ: Education, Inc

Hernandez, M., Eberly, M. B., Avolio, B. J., & Johnson, M. D. (2011). The loci and mechanisms of leadership: Exploring a more comprehensive view of leadership theory. *Journal of Leadership Quarterly*, 22(); 1165-1185. doi: 10.1016/j.leaqua.2011.09.009

Heye, D. (2006). Creativity and innovation: Two key characteristics of the successful 21st century information professional. *Business Information Review, 23*, 252-257. doi: 10.1177/0266382106072255

Hickman, G. R. (2016). *Leading organizations: Perspectives for a new era* (3rd ed.). Thousand Oaks, CA: Sage Publications.

Hjortdahl, M., Ringen, A. H., Naess, A. C., & Wisborg, T. (2009). Leadership is the essential non-technical skill in the trauma team--results of a qualitative study. *Scandinavian Journal of Trauma, Resuscitation and Emergency Medicine*, 17(1); 48. doi: 10.1186/1757-7241-17-48

Ho, L.-A. (2008). What affects organizational performance? The linking of learning and knowledge management. *Journal of Industrial Management & Data Systems* 108; 1234-1254.doi:10.1108/02635570810914919

Hogan, R., & Kaiser, R. B. (2005). What we know about leadership. *Review of General Psychology, 9*, 169-180. doi:10.1037/1089-2680.9.2.169

Holdnak, B. J., Harsh, J., & Bushardt, S. C. (1993). An examination of leadership style and its relevance to shift work in an organizational setting. *Health Care Management Review*, 18(3); 21-30. Doi: 10.1097/00004010-199301830-00003

Holt, S., & Marques, J. (2012). Empathy in leadership: Appropriate or misplaced? An empirical study on a topic that is asking for attention. *Journal of Business Ethics, 105*, 95-105, doi: 10.1007/s10551-011-0951-5

House, R. J., Wright, N. S., & Aditya, R. N. (1997). Cross-cultural research on organizational leadership. In P.C. Earley, & M. Erez (Eds.), *New perspective in international industrial organizational psychology* (pp.535-625). San Francisco, CA: New Lexington.

Howell, J. M., & Avolio, B. J. (1993). Transformational leadership, transactional leadership, locus of control, and support for innovation; key predictors of consolidated business-unit performance. *Journal of Applied Psychology, 78*, 891-902. doi:10.1037/0021-9010.78.6.891

Huq, R. A. (2016). Employee empowerment. *Leadership Excellence Essentials*, 33(2); 38. Retrieved from proquest.com

IBM (2016). SPSS Statistics Version 24. Retrieved from https://ecampus. phoenix.edu/secure/AAPD/vendors/IBM/

Islam, M. R., Rasul, M. T., & Ullah, G. W. (2012). Analysis of the factors that affect job satisfaction: A case study on private companies' employees of Bangladesh. *European Journal of Business and Management,* 4(4). Retrieved from http://www.iiste.org

Jinyun, D., Chenwei, L., Yue, X., & Chia-huei, W. (2016). Transformational leadership and employee voice behavior: A Pygmalion mechanism: A Pygmalion Mechanism. *Journal of Organizational Behavior,* 38(5); 650-670. doi:10.1002/job.2157

Johnson, D.R., & Creech, J.C. (1983). Ordinal measures in multiple indicator models: A simulation study of categorization error. *American Sociological Review,* 48(3), 398-407. doi: 10.2307/2095231

Johnson, P. & Duberley, B. (2001). *Understanding management research: An introduction to epistemology.* Thousand Oaks, CA: Sage Publications.

Johnson, R. (2017).*5different types of leadership styles.* Retrieved fromhttp://smallbusiness.chron.com/5-different-types-leadership-styles-17584.html

Jones, G. R. (2013). *Organizational theory, design, and change* (7ᵗʰedition). Upper Saddle River, NJ:.

Judge, T. A., & Piccolo, R. F. (2004). Transformational and transactional leadership: A meta-analytic test of their relative validity. *Journal of Applied Psychology,* 89(5), 755-768. doi: 10.1037/0021-9010.89.5.755

Kaur, S. P. (2013). Variables in research. *Indian Journal of Research and Reports in Medical Sciences,* 3(4), 36-38 Retrieved from http://www.ijrrms.com

Keith, T. Z. (2015). Multiple regression and beyond: An introduction to multiple regression and structural equation modeling, Kindle Edition Retrieved from http://tzkeith.com/

Kirkbride, P. (2006). Developing transformational leaders: the full range leadership model in action. *Industrial and Commercial Training, 38,* 23-33. doi:10.1108/00197850610646016

Kirkman, B. L., & Shapiro, D. L. (2001). The impact of cultural values on job satisfaction and organizational commitment in self-managing work team: The mediating role of employee resistance. *Academy of Management Journal, 44*(3), 557-569. doi: 10.2307/3069370.

Kirkpatrick, S. A., & Locke, E. A. (1991). Leadership: Do traits really matter? *Academy of Management Executive, 5 (2)*, 48-60. Retrieved from https://sites.fas.harvard.edu

Knupfer, N. N., & McLellan, H. (2001). Descriptive research methodologies. In D. H. Jonassen (Ed.), *Handbook of research for educational communications and technology.* Bloomington, IN: AECT.

Kuhn, T. S. (2012). *The structure of scientific revolutions: Revolutions as changes of world view* (2nd ed.). Chicago, IL: The University of Chicago Press.

Laerd Statistics (2018). 's correlation using stata. Retrieved from https://statistics.laerd.com/stata-tutorials/s-correlation-using-stata.php

Leach, L. S. (2005). Nurse executive transformational leadership and organizational commitment. *Journal of Nursing Administration, 35*(5), 228-237. doi: 10.1097/00005110-200505000-00006

Leedy, P. D., & Ormrod, J. E. (2013). *Practical Research: planning and design.* (10th ed.). Education, Inc.

Levitt, S. D., & List, J. A. (2011). Was there really a Hawthorne effect at the Hawthorne plant? An analysis of the original illumination experiments. *American Economic Journal: Applied Economics*, 3(1); 224–238 Retrieved from http://home.uchicago.edu

Lindebaum, D., & Fielden, S. (2011). 'It's good to be angry': Enacting anger in construction project management to achieve perceived leader effectiveness. Human Relations, Sage Publications, 64(3); 437-458. doi: 10.1177/0018726710381149

Livingston, J. S. (2003, January). Pygmalion in management. *Harvard Business Review, 81*, 97-106. Retrieved from www.hbr.org

Locke, E.A. & Lathan, G.P. (1976). *Theory of goal setting and task performance.* Englewood Cliffs, N.J.: Prentice-Hall.

Maxwell, J. C. (2013). *How successful people lead: Taking your influence to the next level. New York, NY: Center Street*

Mayhew, R. (2014). What are the causes of workplace conflict? Retrieved from http://yourbusiness.azcentral.com/causes-workplace-conflict-3765.htm

McGregor, D. (1960). *The human side of enterprise.* New York, NY: McGraw Hill.

Memoona, Z., Kiran, R., & Bahaudin, G. M. (2015. Impact of transactional, transformational and laissez-faire leadership styles on motivation: a quantitative study of banking employees in Pakistan. *Public Organization Review, 15*(4); 531-549. doi.org/10.1007/s11115-014-0287-6

Menard, S. (2009). *Logistic regression: From introductory to advanced concepts and applications.* Thousand Oaks, CA: Sage Publications

Meyer, J. P., Srinivas, E. S., Lal, J. B., & Topolnytsky, L. (2007). Employee commitment and support for an organizational change: Test of the three-component model in two cultures. *Journal of Occupational and Organizational Psychology, 80*, 185-211. doi: 10.1348/096317906X118685

Meyers, L. S., Gamst, G., & Guarino, A. J. (2013). *Applied multivariate research: Design and implementation (2nd ed.).* Thousand Oaks, CA: SAGE Publications, Inc.

Michel, J. W., Lyons, B. D., & Cho, J. (2011). Is the full-range model of leadership really a full-range model of effective leader behavior? *Journal of Leadership & Organizational Studies, 18*(4), 492-507. doi:10.1177/1548051810377764

Mobbs, C. W. (2011). What are innovation audits? http://www.innovationforgrowth.co.uk/resources/What-are-innovation-audits.pdf

Morrison, R. S., Jones, L., & Fuller, B. (1997). The relation between leadership style and empowerment on job satisfaction of nurses. *Journal of Nursing Administration, 27*(5), 27-34. doi:10.1097/00005110-199705000-00007

Mumford. D., Todd, E. M., Higgs, C., & McIntosh, T. (2017).Cognitive skills and leadership performance: The nine critical skills. *The Leadership Quarterly*, 28(1); 24-39. doi: 10.1016/j.leaqua.2016.10.012

Muogbo, U. S. (2013). The impact of employee motivation on organizational performance: A study of some selected firms in Anambra State Nigeria. *The International Journal of Engineering and Science,* 2(7); 70-80. Retrieved from http://theijes.com

Naismith, N., Sethi, R., Hoseini, A. G., & Tookey, J. (2016). Managing conflict in engineering projects: New Zealand experiences. *International Journal of Construction Supply Chain Management,* 6(1), 19-34. doi: 10.14424/ijcscm601016-19-34

Neuman, W. L. (2011). *Social research methods: Qualitative and quantitative approaches* (7th ed.). Boston, MA: Allyn & Bacon.

Newton, R.R., & Rudestam, K.E. (2013). *Your statistical consultant: Answers to your data analysis questions.* Thousand Oaks, CA: SAGE Publications

Noe, J. (2012). The relationship between principal's emotional intelligence quotient, school culture, and student achievement ProQuest *Dissertations Publishing, 3546183.* Retrieved from Proquest.com

Nonaka, I., & Nishiguchi, T. (2001). Emergence of "Ba": A conceptual framework for the continuous self-transcending process of knowledge creation. In I. Nonaka, & T. Nishiguchi (Eds.), *Knowledge emergence* (pp. 13-29). Oxford, UK: Oxford University Press.

O'Dwyer, L. M., & Bernauer, J. A. (2014). *Quantitative research for the qualitative researcher.* Thousand Oaks, CA: Sage.

Ojokuku, R. M., Odetayo, T. A., & Sajuyigbe, S. A. (2012). Impact of leadership style on organizational performance: A case study of Nigerian banks. *American Journal of Business and Management, 1 (4),* 201-207. doi: https://doi.org/10.11634/216796061706212

Osborne, J. W., & Waters, E. (2002). Four assumptions of multiple regressions that researchers should always test. *Journal of Practical Assessment, Research, and Evaluation,* 8(2), 1-9 Retrieved from http://pareonline.net

Parand, A., Dopson, S., & Vincent, C. (2013). The role of chief executive officers in a quality improvement initiative: a qualitative study. *BMJ Open; London, 3*(1). doi:10.1136/bmjopen-2012-00131

Payne, S. C., & Huffman, A. H. (2005). A longitudinal examination of the influence of mentoring on organizational commitment and turnover. *Academy of Management Journal, 48*(1), 158-168. doi: 10.5465/AMJ.2005.15993166

Ponto, J. (2015). Understanding and evaluating survey research. *Journal of the Advanced Practitioners in Oncology, 6*(2), 168-171. Retrieved from https://www.ncbi.nlm.nih.gov/pmc/articles/PMC4601897/

Razali, N. M., & Wah, Y. B. (2011). Power comparisons of shapiro-wilk, kolmogorov-smirnov, lilliefors and Anderson-darling tests. *Journal of Statistical Modeling and Analytics, 2*(1), 21-33.

Riley, T., & Ungerleider, C. (2012). Self-fulfilling prophecy: How teachers' attributions, expectations, and stereotypes influence the learning opportunities afforded aboriginal students. *Canadian Journal of Education, 35*(2), 303-333. Retrieved from https://eric.ed.gov

Rogelberg, S. G. (Ed.). (2004). *Handbook of research methods in industrial and organizational psychology.* Malden, MA: Blackwell Publishing, Ltd

Rosenberg, M. J., & Hovland, C. I. (1960). Cognitive, affective, and behavioral components of attitudes. In M. J. Rosenberg, C. I. Hovland, W. J. McGuire, R. P. Abelson & J. W. Brehm, (Eds.), *Attitude organization and change: An analysis of consistency among attitude components* (pp. 1-14). New Haven, CT: Yale University Press.

Rowold, J. (2005). Multifactor leadership questionnaire. *Mind Garden, Inc.* Retrieved from http://www.mindgarden.com/documents/MLQGermanPsychometric.pdf

Ruiz, P., Ruiz, C., & Martínez, R. (2011). Improving the "leader-follower" relationship: Top manager or supervisor? The ethical leadership trickle-down effect on follower job response. *Journal of Business Ethics, 99*, 587-608. doi:10.1007/s10551-010-0670-3

Sankey, K. S., & Machin, M. A. (2014). Employee participation in non-mandatory professional development – the role of core proactive motivation processes. *International journal of training and development,* 18(4); 241-255. doi:10.1111/ijtd.12036

Sarros, J. C., Luca, E., Densten, I., & Santora, J. C. (2014). Leaders and their use of motivating language. *Leadership & Organization Development Journal.* 35, 226-240.doi:10.1108/LODJ-06-2012-0073

Schin, G., & Racovita, M. (2013). The influence of dominant leadership styles on employees' behavior: Empirical evidence from the Romanian public institution. *Contemporary Readings in Law and Social Justice,* 5 (2), 777-785. Retrieved fromhttps://www.questia.com

Schommer-Aikins, M., & Hutter, R. (2002). Epistemological beliefs and thinking about everyday controversial issues. *Journal of Psychology,* 136, 5-20. doi:10.1080/00223980209604134

Scott, J., Revera, M. D., McRitchie, A., Riviello, R., Smink, D., & Yule, S. (2016). Non-technical skills and health care provision in low- and middle-income countries: a systematic review. *Journal of Medical Education,* 50(4); 441-455.doi:10.111/medu.12939

Scott, W. R., & Davis, G. F. (2007). *Organizations and organizing: Rational, natural, and open system perspectives.* New York, NY: Taylor & Francis.

Sergiovanni, T. J. (1990). Adding value to leadership gets extraordinary results. *Educational leadership,* 47(8), 23-27. Retrieved from www. ascd.org/publications/educational-leadership.aspx

Seteroff, S. S. (2006). *Beyond leadership to followership: Learning to lead from where you are.* Victoria, Canada: Trafford Publishing.

Shamir, B., & Howell, J. M. 1999). Organizational and contextual influences on the emergence and effectiveness of charismatic leadership. *Leadership Quarterly,* 10(2), 257-283. doi: 10.1016/ S1048-9843(99)00014-4

Simons, T., Leroy, H., Collewaert, V., & Masschelein, S. (2015). How leader alignment of words and deeds affects followers: A meta-analysis of behavioral integrity research. Journal of Business Ethics, 132(4); 831-844. doi: 10.1007/s10551-014-2332-3

Skovholt, K., Gronning, A., & Kankaanranta, A. (2014). The communicative functions of emoticons in workplace e-mails. *Journal of Computer-Mediated Communication, 19*(4); 780-797. doi: 10.1111/jcc4.12063

Soper, D. (2015). *Statistics calculators*: Version 3.0. Retrieved from http://danielsoper.com/statcalc3/calc.aspx?id=1

Sproul, N. L. (2002). *Handbook of research methods: A guide for practitioners and students in the social sciences* (2nd ed.). Lanham, MD: Scarecrow Press, Inc.

Srivastava, T. (2015, June 17). What's the difference between causality and correlation? Retrieved from https://www.analyticsvidhya.com/blog/2015/06/establish-causality-events/

Statistics Canada Catalogue no. 12-591-X. Ottawa. Version updated May 2009. Ottawa./pub/12-591-x/12-591-x2009001-eng.htm Accessed February 14, 2018.

Stevens, J. P. (2009). *Applied multivariate statistics for the social sciences* (5th ed.). Mahwah, NJ: Routledge Academic.

Sullivan, G. M., & Artino Jr, A. R. (2013). Analyzing and interpreting data from Likert-type scales. *Journal of graduate medical education, 5*(4), 541-542. doi: 10.4300/JGME-5-4-18

Sultana, N. (2012). Gender comparison of administrative skills at secondary schools' level. *Journal of Educational Research, 15*(2), 65-71. Retrieved from https://www.questia.com

Thietart, R-A., & Wauchope, S. (2001). *Doing management research: A comprehensive guide.* Thousand Oaks, CA: Sage Publications, Inc.

Thompson, L. L. (2014). *Making the team: A guide for managers* (5th ed.). Upper Saddle River, NJ:.

Tidd, J., & Bessant, J. (2013). *Managing innovation: Integrating technology, market and organizational change* (5th ed.). West Sussex, UK: John Wiley & Sons, Inc.

Tohidi, H.&Jabbari, M. M. (2012). Innovation as a success key for organizations. *Procedia Technology, 1*(), *560-564.* https://doi.org/10.1016/j.protcy.2012.02.122

Tsoukas, H. (2005). *Complex knowledge: Studies in organizational epistemology.* New York, NY: Oxford

USC Libraries Research Guides, (2017, August 28). Organizing your social sciences research paper: independent and dependent variables. Retrieved from http://libguides.usc.edu/writingguide/variables

Vecchio, R. P. (1988). *Organizational behavior.* (2nd ed.) Chicago, IL: Dryden.

Vecchio, R. P., & Fernandez, C. F. (2002). Leading people and organizations.

Walumbwa, F. O., Orwa, B., Wang, P., & Lawler, L. J. (2005). Transformational leadership, organizational commitment, and job satisfaction: A comparative study of Kenyan and U.S. financial firms. Human Resource Development Quarterly, 16(2), 235-256. doi: 10.1002/hrdq.1135

White, M. A., & Bruton, G. D. (2011). *The management of technology and innovation: A strategic approach* (2nd ed.). Mason, OH: South-Western Cengage Learning.

Wren, J. T. (1995). *Leader's Companion: Insights on leadership through the ages.* New York, NY: The Free Press.

Yang, M. L. (2012). Transformational leadership and Taiwanese public relations practitioners' job satisfaction and organizational commitment. *Social Behavior and Personality: An International Journal,* 40(1), 31-46. doi:10.2224/sbp.2012.40.1.31

Yukl, G. A. (2013). *Leadership in Organizations,* (8th ed.). New York, NY:

Zhuplatova, I. (2015). A correlational study of transformational and transactional leadership and organizational commitment in small entrepreneurial firms. Retrieved from Dissertation & Theses. Proquest.com

Zumbo, B.D., & Zimmerman, D.W. (1993). Is the selection of statistical methods governed by level of measurement? *Canadian Psychology Association, 34*(4), 390-400.doi: 10.1037/h0078865

www.ingramcontent.com/pod-product-compliance
Lightning Source LLC
Chambersburg PA
CBHW030812180526
45163CB00003B/1253